Ecclesia

2

St Macarius Press

©2025 St Macarius Press

Monastery of Saint Macarius the Great
(Egypt)
P.O. Box 2780
Cairo—Egypt

Website: www. stmacariuspress.com
Telegram Channel: t.me/stmacariuspress
Facebook page: www.facebook.com/stmacariuspress
Twitter: @stmacariuspress

Our Address in the USA:
13303 Scotch Run Ct
Centreville, VA 20120-6428
United States of America

All rights reserved.

MATTHEW THE POOR

THE MYSTERY OF UNITY

WRITINGS ON ECUMENISM

FOREWORD BY
VASSILIKI STATHOKOSTA

INTRODUCTION BY
MONK WADID EL MACARI

TRANSLATION FROM ARABIC BY
ANDREW N A YOUSSEF

EDITION AND REVISION BY
MONKS OF THE MONASTERY OF SAINT MACARIUS

ST MACARIUS PRESS
MONASTERY OF SAINT MACARIUS THE GREAT (EGYPT)

ISBN
978-1-7350713-9-8

Library of Congress Control Number
2024939910

Series
Ecclesia

Foreword
Vassiliki Stathokosta

Introduction
Monk Wadid el Macari

Translation from Arabic
Andrew N A Youssef

Edition and Revision
Monks of the Monastery of St. Macarius

Cover
David Georgy

Format
5" x 8"

Pages
87

Second Revised Reprint—June 2025

CONTENTS

Foreword by V. Stathokosta   7

Introduction by Monk Wadid el Macari   11

Prayer   23

Christian Unity   25

One Christ and One Holy, Catholic Church   39

True Unity will be an Inspiration for the World   49

In the Meaning of Unity: Will These Days Return?   83

FOREWORD

I was blessed to read *The Mystery of Unity: Writings on Ecumenism* as soon as I received a digital copy via the internet. That very moment, I felt once again the richness of the tradition of the Orthodox family and our common longing for visible unity, as the author, Fr. Matthew the Poor, exposed in his texts, full of spirituality and theological depth. I refer to the Orthodox family as meaning the two church traditions, the Eastern Orthodox and the Oriental Orthodox, although we are separated and have lived apart for many centuries. Since 451, that is, since the fourth Synod in Chalcedon, we are not in communion. Nevertheless, we both believe in the Triune God, and we confess the Creed of Nicaea-Constantinople. Our Lord's prayer "that they may be one in us" (John 17:21) urges us, Eastern and Oriental Orthodox, to find ways to overcome the trauma of separation and to walk together, united in the one faith and living in the One, Holy, Catholic, and Apostolic Church.

The modern ecumenical movement that started to develop at the beginning of the twentieth century enabled Eastern Orthodox churches and Oriental Orthodox churches to meet and act as one Church family. When representatives of Eastern Orthodox and Oriental Orthodox churches met at the second Conference of Faith and Order in Edinburgh, UK, in August 1937, they had fruitful cooperation. Thus, the Greek Orthodox asked the Orientals to present them with their faith, their order, and their liturgical life. They also suggested they get in touch with Constantinople's Ecumenical

Patriarchate. It is noteworthy that a great figure of the Ecumenical Movement, the Greek Prof. Amilkas Alivizatos, referred to the Oriental Churches not as "Monophysites" but as "Old Orthodox," paying them great respect.

The Eastern Orthodox Churches expressed in 1920 their eagerness for church unity in the Encyclical Letter issued by the Ecumenical Patriarchate addressed "unto the Churches of Christ everywhere" for cooperation and dialogue.[1] The Ecumenical Patriarchate of Constantinople felt it was his great duty to work for the unity of the Church. That great duty for church unity is described by Fr. Matthew the Poor as a vital need for the Christian believer: "The Christian person seeks unity as he seeks God,"[2] giving at the same time the very characteristic of the Christian faith as "Christian unity is first and foremost a demand of faith, and we plead for it because it is demanded of us in our hearts."[3] Unity is a strong will, desire, condition, and the status quo that a Christian believer wishes to be united with the Triune God and with humans. Unity is the cornerstone on which Christian faith is based. However, inevitably, one could ask, what about love, as love is the quintessence of the teaching of Jesus? Here comes the connection of love and unity, as Fr. Matthew explained: "The Christian person seeks unity as he seeks God."[4] That means that unity is motivated by love—love and unity go together—one is the seed, and the other is the fruit. Love

---

[1] The English version can be found in G. K. A. Bell, *Documents on Christian Unity 1920–1930* (London: Oxford University Press, 1955): 17–21.

[2] *Infra*: 25.

[3] *Infra*: 25.

[4] *Infra*: 25.

unites us with God and with all his creation because "the path that leads unto union with God is not a one-way path that ends with God alone as the final destination. Instead, it leads back toward the neighbor, the stranger, the sojourner, the enemy, and all of creation."[5]

In this book, the reader is given the possibility to study a very well-organized exposition on the presuppositions, the terms, and the method of dialogue that aims for the unity of all. But mostly those two concepts of love and unity, which are often misunderstood, are explained by Fr. Matthew the Poor. Love is not a sentimental situation but a deeply spiritual experience. Thus, "one of the most dangerous matters that can happen is to let emotions creep into and permeate our quest for Christian unity."[6] Likewise, unity "is not an emotional condescension… It is a divine drawing, more than a human effort."[7]

Still, there are multiple obstacles to unity that keep churches apart. Fr. Matthew dares to name loud and clear certain obstacles to inter-Christian dialogue as the ones stated in his deep prayer to God, such as "political, ideological, and ethnical fights" that we elevate "above the needs of the spirit, faith, and love."[8] In a prophetic warning, he condemned the phenomenon of secularization, saying that "we hushed the voice of Christ in our hearts to please the world and the

---

[5] *Infra*: 28.
[6] *Infra*: 27.
[7] *Infra*: 28.
[8] *Infra*: 24.

people."[9] But "any hindrance in fulfilling the unity that You plead for all of us is a failure of faith and a lack of love."[10]

Another mistake that keeps us apart is in the method of dialogue, "trying to lift sin by sin or healing sickness by sickness"[11] and "to seek unity through ideological fights, or through associating love with politics, and do not allow that they may be deceived by ethnic coalitions, perceiving them to be a spiritual force."[12]

Fr. Matthew wrote as if he prayed to God, preached love and unity, taught spirituality, and were a prophet, bringing judgment as well as hope for the people of God. Readers may pray with him and follow his thoughts till his conclusion that "regardless of how we put the responsibility of unity on the Church, it falls at the end on the shoulders of the saints. If we seek a prompt start, our eyes are fixed on the chosen and gifted in every church, no matter how much they hide to disappear from the center stage."[13]

Vassiliki Stathokosta
Associate Professor for Orthodox Theology and the Ecumenical Movement
Theological School, National and Kapodistrian University of Athens, Greece

---

[9] *Ibid.*
[10] *Ibid.*
[11] *Infra*: 24.
[12] *Ibid.*
[13] *Infra*: 81.

INTRODUCTION

Understanding the Church as the completion of the Incarnation, that is, the union of divine and human nature, is a prerequisite for comprehending Fr. Matthew the Poor's views on Christian unity.

On this, Fr. Matthew wrote:

> The Church was revealed for the first time in the incarnation of the Son. The union of divinity and humanity is in fact the prototype, the deeper meaning, and the full reality of the Church—the Assembly of God with humanity. Also, the manifestation of God in a human body was the first revelation of the nature of the Church, and the actualization of her existence on earth. The Holy Spirit was the agent of this mysterious union between the divine and the human [...] It is quite evident that the divine body of Christ is itself the Church: "And He put all *things* under His feet, and gave Him *to be* head over all *things* to the Church, which is His body, the fullness of Him who fills all in all." (Eph. 1:22-23).[1]

While for many exegetes the expression "the Church is the body of Christ" is an image or an allegory, for Fr. Matthew—as for many Church Fathers—it is a mystical reality, which is to say, one that defies sensory and rational comprehension but remains real, indeed more real than the realities of this world. This mystical reality is based on the gift that the Lord gave us on the evening of Maundy Thursday: He gave us His

---

[1] Mattā al-Miskīn, *al-'Anṣara* [The Pentecost] (Wādī al-Naṭrūn: Monastery of St. Macarius, 1960): 15.

body and His blood so, by uniting with Him, we might become "members of His body, of His flesh and of His bones"[2] (Eph. 5:30), a favorite verse of Fr. Matthew that he never failed to quote in his writings on the Church.

The Incarnation, the Eucharist, and the Church are various aspects of the same reality, that of the greatest gift the Creator could bestow upon His creation.[3] He gave Himself to us to make us "members of His body, of His flesh, and of His bones." On this gift the angels "lean with desire" (cf. 1 Pet. 1:12), because the Lord did not unite Himself with their nature, but He united Himself with ours to make us members of His body. Seeing what we have done with this extraordinary gift—the gift of His body, whose members He made us and how we have torn it apart without pity—the angels are astonished. More than once, Fr. Matthew confided to his close disciples:

> When the division of the Church is observed, the angels shed tears. This constitutes the most egregious transgression the creature has ever committed against his Creator; it is an offense in return for the most magnificent gift the Creator ever bestowed upon His creation.

---

[2] It is notable that this term "of His flesh and bones," although absent from the manuscripts of the fourth century, is already found in the second century in St. Irenaeus of Lyon (Adv. Haer. 4:16) and in important editions such as the Old Latin and Vulgate and the Syriac New Testament.

[3] Fr. Matta wrote an article entitled "Christ, God's Free Gift to Humanity," cf. Matthew the Poor, *Love Took Flesh: Nativity Letters* (Wādī al-Naṭrūn: St Macarius Press, 2021): 37.

It is in this light that we must understand certain allusions of Fr. Matthew to his own interior life and his tearful prayer for unity:

> Christian unity is the ultimate quest of faith to the extent that it overflows in our being and causes our hearts and emotions to vibrate. We seek unity with tears, for we seek Christ.[4]

> Now, with great yearning, tears, prayers, and the consciousness of the new man, we look forward to the fulfillment of the catholicity and unity of the Church in the whole world.[5]

The immense gravity of the "crime of division" stems from the Church's identification with Christ's body.

> [Members of the present] church have mutually accused, condemned, excommunicated, harmed, and cursed one another, while all claim to serve the blessed Name, worship in spirit and truth, and follow the Lord with all their hearts, and at the end God's people pay the price! Christ's heart is pierced, His whole body bleeds and suffers, but everyone remains insensitive, indifferent to this crime committed against Christ, His body and His name.[6]

> It is as if Christ, because of these divisions, is dead, hidden from the world as a buried man in the coldness of

---

[4] *Infra*: 50.

[5] It is with this sentence that the article *One Christ and one Catholic Church* ends. Matthew the Poor, *The Mystery of Unity* (Wādī al-Naṭrūn: St Macarius Press, 2023): 50.

[6] Mattā al-Miskīn, *al-Inğīl biḥasab al-qiddīs Marqus: dirāsa wa-tafsīr wa-šarḥ* (The Gospel according to St. Mark: study, interpretation, and commentary) 9:38 (Wādī al-Naṭrūn: Monastery of St. Macarius, 2020[4]): 424.

animosities and divisions among the churches. Christ waits, and the world waits along with Him, for the end of these divisions, that the warmth of love may spread and, through its spreading, Christ may rise and give life that all may see Him and the world may live on and not die.[7]

Likewise, it is in the light of the Church's identification with the body of Christ that we can understand why Fr. Matthew's quest for unity is identified with the quest for God.

> The Christian person seeks unity as he seeks God. Inasmuch as he is aware of God, he will be aware of the unity in his spirit.[8]
>
> Unity is by no means a matter that can be examined theoretically. Unity is essentially of a divine nature [...] It cannot be seen outside or apart from God.[9]

This is why the cause of unity is crucially that of "the presence of the Lord" in the midst of the assemblies that discuss unity:

> The matter of unity decisively and sharply concerns the presence of the Lord. Through this presence, in fact, unity will divinely take place, and distinctions will be removed. The Lord alone can make "the two into one" and "break down the middle wall of separation" (Eph. 2:14).[10]
>
> When Christ becomes present amidst the debating community then the debate must cease—each one ought to fill his or her eyes and heart with the true unity and prepare

---

[7] *Infra*: 73.
[8] *Infra*: 25.
[9] *Infra*: 29.
[10] *Infra*: 33.

the whole of their inner being to receive and accord that unity. Any question about unity that is posed on the objective theological plane and remains without a solution is in itself sufficient evidence that the Lord is not present amidst the community. This absence of the Lord proves with certainty that the scope of the meeting, the research methods, and the intention of those gathered ought to be re-examined.[11]

The originality of Fr. Matthew manifests itself in a particular way when he considers 'where to start' the path to unity. Already in his first writing on Christian Unity in 1965, he commented on Ephesians 2:14: "For He Himself is our peace, who has made both one, and has broken down the middle wall of separation." Commenting on this, he wrote:

> The case is twofold: first, unity and removing of distinctions on the level of "love the Lord, your God," and second, "love your neighbor." Human logic dictates that the distinctions be removed first for unity to take place. As expressed through divine inspiration (cf. Eph. 2:14), God's logic requires that unity should be accomplished first, so that the middle wall of separation would be broken down.[12]

Unity must be experienced spiritually among Christians before discussing it. This would lead Fr. Matthew in 1984 to advocate courageously for the lifting of anathemas and the resumption of communion from the same chalice between Chalcedonian Orthodox and non-Chalcedonians *before* discussing the details of ecclesial life.

> In this way, as we are united in spirit in God's love and the communion of the Holy Spirit, the One Christ will oblige

---

[11] *Infra*: 32.
[12] *Infra*: 33.

us, or rather inspire us, to acquire one mind, one word, and one utterance. Each Church will not lose her theological formulations and distinct characteristics which are the very same characteristics of the One Christ who lives in her.[13]

The lifting of anathemas and the resumption of communion from the same chalice, in his view, is the only way out of the rigidness of the division. Otherwise, he believes:

> If we start with the canons, it will seem to us, in their light, that we are always right and possess the definite truth while the other is always wrong. We get trapped in this axis of thought, going in circles, until time—and with it, life—will slip away from us.[14]

Whether we suspect it or not, the main obstacle to unity is the 'ego,' both the personal 'ego' and the ecclesial 'ego.' For Father Matthew,

> The ego is, in essence, the source of all the fragmentation that exists in the whole world, and particularly in the Church [...]. Theanthropic unity requires the stripping of the individualistic and collective ego.[15]

> Indeed, if we lift the individual ego and the ecclesial ego from our conscious and subconscious, unity will definitely come to reality.[16]

The renunciation of the personal 'ego' is a scriptural commandment: "If anyone desires to come after Me, let him deny himself, and take up his cross, and follow Me" (Matt.

---

[13] *Infra*: 54.
[14] *Infra*: 51.
[15] *Infra*: 28.
[16] *Infra*: 32.

16:24). This commandment, which is addressed to all Christians, is lived especially in monastic life. It is in this perspective that Fr. Matthew attributed to monastics a particular role in the search for unity, not on the visible plane, but on the invisible plane, that of the struggle which is not against flesh and blood, but against the evil spirits that inhabit the heavenly spaces (cf. Eph. 6:12).

Regarding this matter, he referenced the story concerning a pagan priest who underwent a sudden transformation from paganism to monasticism after overhearing the demons conspire amongst themselves: "Each time we sow discord among the monks, they make *metanoias* against one another; thus, they undermine our influence on the world"[17]

As for the ecclesial 'ego,' it is much more difficult to expunge, since no one is authorized to do so. In 1965, Fr. Matthew wrote:

> Yet, no individual, no matter how great his control over himself may be, can abandon the ecclesial ego with all its traditional, dialectical, canonical, and sacred traits. Even if we are the representatives of our churches, we cannot give up the ego of our churches.[18]

But in 1984, he would say with more assurance:

> Therefore, we are missing the Church, which can behave in the manner Christ behaved: deny herself, carry her cross, and die to the sin of division, that she may live and cause others to live with her [...]. This is to say we ought to move forward with the Spirit of our

---

[17] Cf. *Bustān*: apothegm n. 1162 (cf. Anba Epiphanius (ed.), *Bustān al-ruhbān* (Wādī al-Naṭrūn: Monastery of St. Macarius, 2013), 429).

[18] *Infra*: 32.

> Lord Jesus, where each church carries the sins of the other church upon itself concurrently and reciprocally. We say: 'Let each church carry the sins of the other church,' without adding anything more.[19]

The meaning of this last expression is unclear, but we believe that it must be understood in the light of the first subtitle of the same article: 'Doctrines are Untouchable.' It is not a question of renouncing one's own convictions, but "that each Church takes upon herself the faults of the other," or instead what she considered to be faulty in the other and accept that defect as valid for the other Church, "without adding anything more," that is to say without renouncing her own formulation.

Accepting that the conviction of the other is *valid for him* is a theme to which Fr. Matthew returns, not in a relativistic sense—as if the truth would have no intrinsic existence—but in the sense that this mutual benevolent attitude is the best thing we can do to allow Christ the opportunity to perfect our unity in Himself.

> We are not asked now to establish the unity of dogma or the common expression of all the articles of faith, but to accept one another (cf. Rom 15:7) with a sincere love from the bottom of the heart considering that the conviction of the other is *true for him* and that he has sincere faith which is *true for him*. This is what will give Christ, present in our midst, the opportunity to use the power of His presence. The reconciliation of the churches and their agreement in parleys about faith in view of achieving the unity of dogma is an enterprise which exceeds our human capacities. But it is not possible for all to be assembled in the

---

[19] *Infra*: 76.

presence of Christ without Christ unifying faith and dogma by His presence. For what man has damaged cannot be repaired by man, but it belongs to the nature of Christ, it is His specific work, to reconcile the opposites and to make a unity out of two (Cf. Eph. 2:14).[20]

Accepting the other in his peculiarity and convictions that differ from our own is a challenging endeavor. A significant level of self-sacrifice is necessary. This point can only be reached through an immense love for Christ and profound suffering in the midst of the division of His body. Fr. Matthew demonstrated this reality in one of his unrecorded conversations by referencing the 1 Kings 3:16 account of two harlots who argued over the same baby, each asserting that it was her own. Solomon, endowed with extraordinary wisdom, issued the command to divide the child in half, allocating one half to each woman. Then, in tears, the biological mother begged that the baby be given to the other woman without being cut in two. Fr. Matthew perceived it as an emblematic representation of the present state of the contested churches. Who would have a greater love for the Lord than for herself, to the extent that she would be willing to be deemed erroneous (even though she would be right) in order to save the Lord's body from torn apart or cut.

The quest for unity was not for Fr. Matthew a problem among others. By reading the following pages we will be able to see what a preponderant place Christian unity occupied in his life. Even before engaging in monastic life, he was

---

[20] Mattā al-Miskīn, *al-Inǧīl biḥasab al-qiddīs Lūqā: dirāsa wa-tafsīr wa-šarḥ* (The Gospel according to St. Luke: study, interpretation, and commentary), 9:49 (Wādī al-Naṭrūn: Monastery of St. Macarius, 2020⁴): 472.

predisposed to this quest by his openness towards Christians of other denominations and even members of other religions, an exceptional openness for a Coptic youth of that time. This incident testifies this attitude that he recounts in his autobiography.

> One evening, I was shocked when we were gathered in the house of Sa'd Aziz (who later became Bishop Samuel) in Giza. During this friendly meeting, one of the participants raised a question about our relations with the Protestants. A Sunday School leader responded in a way that made it clear that we were not to have any dealings with them. I started wondering why. The discussion evolved, resulting in the following response: 'We should only reach out to those who share our beliefs.' I protested that this would lead to isolation and was not in line with the Gospel. Then in my turn I asked an embarrassing but decisive question: 'Will Protestants and Catholics enter the kingdom of God?' The chief of the assembly [...] took up my question and asked everyone to answer it in turn. There were about twenty young men there. The unanimous answer was that obviously neither Protestants nor Catholics would enter the kingdom, otherwise what would be the value of Orthodoxy? I realized then that I was in the presence of a religious, civil, and social catastrophe. But from this survey, I began to understand the realities around me.[21]

Throughout his monastic life, his interest in the unity, not only of the Church, but of all humanity in God did not cease to increase. To the extent that the quest for unity was identified for him with the quest for God, insofar as that his love for the Church was identified with his love for Christ

---

[21] Mattā al-Miskīn, *al-Sīra al-ḏātiyya* (Autobiography), (Wādī al-Naṭrūn: Monastery of St. Macarius, 2006), 7-8.

whose body she is. This love, has occupied a central place in his spiritual life.

And this continued until his last years. When his state of health no longer allowed him to read easily, he spent his hours sitting in his chair meditating gently. He then asked one of his close disciples to bring him a reproduction of the painting of the Last Supper that he cherished so much, and of which he had illustrated in more than one of his books, and to hang it on the wall in front of him. He spent his long hours meditating the communion with *the Twelve*.[22]

To understand the significance of this fact, one must know what 'the Twelve' meant to him. By gleaning from his various books, one could gather an important insight on this subject. Here are some examples:

> The 'Twelve' is not a mere number but contains the Church herself, a single body submitted to a single Head.[23]
>
> The unity of the Church is the new creation represented by 'the Twelve.'[24]
>
> The 'Twelve' continues to represent in our minds how Christ chose them to make them the new-born Church. The Church is not the heir of the 'Twelve,' but she is herself the

---

[22] Carl Bloch, *The Last Supper* (oil on copper plate), late 19th century, Castle of Frederiksborg, Denmark.

[23] Mattā al-Miskīn, *Šarḥ inğīl al-qiddīs Yūḥānnā* (Commentary on the Gospel of St. John), 6:70 (Wādī al-Naṭrūn: Monastery of St. Macarius, 2018⁵): 470.

[24] Mattā al-Miskīn, *Šarḥ sifr aʿmāl al-rusul: ḥarakat al-kanīsa biqiyādat al-rūḥ al-qudus ʿabr al-duhūr* (Commentary on the book of Acts of the Apostles: the movement of the Church under the guidance of the Holy Spirit throughout the ages), 2:4 (Wādī al-Naṭrūn: Monastery of St. Macarius, 2021⁶): 161.

'Twelve,' the body corporate of Christ Himself.[25]

How can we return to the one and Apostolic Church—that of the "Twelve"—if not by getting rid of hatred and returning to love. For it is certain that each Church holds to the true faith of the 'Twelve.'[26]

And now that Fr. Matthew has joined up in peace with the celestial Church of the "Twelve," the one he has cherished so much throughout his life, may he by his prayers promote the resumption of communion between the various members of this one Church.

> Monk Wadid el Macari
> Monastery of St. Macarius the Great
> (Egypt)
> Feast of Pentecost 2024

---

[25] Mattā al-Miskīn, *al-Inğīl biḥasab al-qiddīs Marqus*: 302.
[26] *Ibid.*, 303.

PRAYER

O Holy Father,[1] who glorified Your Son Jesus, having given Him authority over all flesh to grant eternal life to all who believe in Him as God and Savior. We thank You for You have given us the comprehension of the depth of the mystery of Your divinity and the essential unity between You, Your Son, and Your Holy Spirit. This unity to which we are called by the prayer of Your Son unto You, "that they all may be one, as You, Father, are in Me, and I in You; that they also may be one in Us, that the world may believe that You sent Me" (John 17:21). Truly, we believe that the unity You call us to is a necessity, for it is a witness to the mystery of Your work in human nature, which tends to corruption and fragmentation due to sin and egoism. It is also a necessity so that the world may believe that it has no hope apart from Jesus Christ, Your Beloved One, whom You sent to unite the heavenly to the earthly, the People to the peoples, and the soul

---

[1] Mattā al-Miskīn, *al-Wiḥda al-masīḥiyya* (Wādī al-Naṭrūn: Monastery of Saint Macarius, 2014⁴): 5.

to the body. We confess that the sending of Your Son into our hearts, "that Christ may dwell in your hearts through faith" (Eph. 3:17), was necessarily to create in us an irresistible and immediate inclination toward unity. "I in them, and You in Me; that they may be made perfect in one, and that the world may know that You have sent Me, and have loved them as You have loved Me" (John 17:23). Therefore, any hindrance in fulfilling the unity which You plead for all of us is a failure of faith and a lack of love. Subsequently, we began to elevate political, ideological, and ethnical fights above the needs of spirit, faith, and love. We hushed the voice of Christ in our hearts to please the world and people.

O Holy Father, glorify Your Son in the life of the Church that she may glorify You and Your Son as well. This shall be done when all give up the hindrances of unity and love. Do not permit, O Lord, Your people to stumble, trying to lift sin by sin or healing sickness by sickness. Do not allow them to seek unity through ideological fights, or through associating love with politics, and do not allow that they may be deceived by ethnic coalitions, perceiving them to be a spiritual force. Amen.

CHRISTIAN UNITY

The Christian person seeks unity as he seeks God.[1] Inasmuch as he is aware of God, he will be aware of the unity in his spirit. Christian unity is first and foremost a demand of faith, and we plead for it because it is demanded of us in our hearts. Given that not everyone is aware of God at the same level, unity is not seen from the same angle. It expands and contracts in proportion to the depth of one's genuine relationship with God. Some do not feel the presence of unity at all, while others deny it. All in all, it is a test of faith.

One's predisposition towards unity is, etiologically, tied to a maturity of faith and a profound spirituality that extends beyond the barriers of hate, ideological disagreements, psychological incongruity, mental pretenses, and fleshly cares. Unity between us must be pleaded on a divine plan as it is beyond human ability alone. Unity occurs as a necessity or a direct, inevitable result of the union of humanity with God. Those who live by the Spirit are aware of this spiritual law which is based on an empirical foundation and on the testimony of Scripture in several occasions.

The first commandment for us is, "You shall love the Lord your God with all your heart, with all your soul, and with all your mind." The second is, "You shall love your

---

[1] First published in January 1965. Mattā al-Miskīn, "al-Wiḥda al-masīḥiyya," in *al-Wiḥda al-masīḥiyya fī ḍaw' ma'nā al-kanīsa wa-ḥaqīqat al-masīḥ* (Wādī al-Naṭrūn: Monastery of Saint Macarius, 2014⁴): 6-15.

neighbor as yourself" (Matt. 22:37-39). Scripture here affirms that the second commandment is fulfilled on the basis of the first one since it proceeds from it. The second commandment apart from the first is meaningless and almost sinful.

Therefore, the fact that the churches insist on unity in the present time in which they all complain about the deterioration of faith in the hearts of the shepherds and their flocks, spiritual weakness, and the reluctance of youth to consecrate their life unto the Lord, is a problematic matter. What are, then, the motivations that triggered the insistence on unity to this overwhelming degree? If there were a spiritual awakening and genuine zeal for the faith, unity would be accompanied by collective and individual conversion to God. This would take place in the form of relentless repentance, remorse, and pleading for forgiveness, in a manner similar to how the people of God behaved after a period of lukewarmness or straying. However, such demand for unity to this insistent extent, while we are in such a state of weakness, lukewarmness, and openly estrange ourselves from God, leads us to question ourselves. Whence does such urge come?

Humanity comes originally from one being, Adam. Therefore, it is natural that there is an instinctive longing in us toward natural harmony, which unconsciously stems from emotional inclinations.

Likewise, we live in one world with interests that cooperate sometimes and at other times meet in conflict in a manner that affects our being and life. Thus, another longing came into existence in us towards forming coalitions facing hostile elements. In such cases, we unite against each other.

CHRISTIAN UNITY

First: Unity based on the Emotional Inclination.

One of the most dangerous matters that can happen is to let emotions creep into and permeate our quest for Christian unity. Christian unity requires that we plead for it in a spiritual manner, free from all blemishes of the flesh and emotions: "That which is born of the flesh is flesh, and that which is born of the Spirit is spirit" (John 3:6).

Even when it appears to be good and pure, satisfying the emotions, especially in spiritual matters, cannot fulfill the plea for the truth, as truth ultimately cancels emotions. As the Scripture says: "Those who are in the flesh cannot please God" (Rom. 8:8). Therefore, even though emotions appear to be harmonious with the spirit at the beginning of the path ascending unto the truth, they act as a danger in the path which is sufficient to repel us and prevent us from ascending. Emotions work subconsciously for the flesh. Even when emotions are submitted to the Spirit, they create a forgery that borrows spiritual qualities and exploits them to glorify the ego.

If the unity made by men, even though it is under a spiritual guise, bases itself upon emotions, it serves our own glory and the exaltation of the human ego. God, in the process, will become merely secondary. As a result, the dialogues and negotiations will turn into a "serious" attempt to find a common language that may be used for the mutual understanding of the "men of Babel" to resume building the tower leading to heaven!

The ego is, in essence, the source of all the fragmentation that exists in the whole world, and particularly in the Church.

CHRISTIAN UNITY

God seeks the unity of men so that *He* may be the head—"That they may be one in us" (John 17:21). Theanthropic unity requires the stripping of the individualistic and collective ego. Emotions are the most deceptive form of the ego because they are the closest to the spirit.

Whether my own emotions deceive me or whether the other party desires unity with me for their own ego, the result is similarly bad. I might even give up my ego that the other may be glorified rather than God. In this scenario, my renunciation would be an illusion, for I must give up my own ego and all my emotions entirely in front of God before I attempt to unite with others. In other words, I must comply with the order of the Scriptural commandment in loving God with *all* my heart, *all* my soul, and *all* my mind (cf. Deut. 6:5) that I may be able to love others with a unifying love which does not harm me or the other person.

Unity is not an emotional condescension but rather, it is an ascent free from the egoistic emotionality, an ascent which one does not accomplish of nor through the ego. It is a divine drawing, more than a human effort. By it, we all get together in God, rather than in ourselves: "No one can come to Me unless the Father who sent Me draws him" (John 6:44).

The path that leads to union with God is not a one-way path that ends with God alone as the final destination. Instead, it leads back toward the neighbor, the stranger, the sojourner, the enemy, and all of creation. If we are being united with God, we ought to immediately consider how we can be united with all and ought not to give ourselves rest until this union is fulfilled. The path from and toward God is in our hearts. If Christian unity is not accomplished to this day, it is because:

CHRISTIAN UNITY

a. we seek it before we surrender all of our hearts, souls, and minds to God;

b. we seek it outside ourselves, which is to say that we try to accomplish it objectively rather than subjectively.

To seek unity before we reach the level of complete submission of the heart, soul, and mind unto God leads to an emotional conflict in which we seek unity for ourselves. Or this could lead us to an intellectual deception in which we seek unity for its own sake, as an exigence that the logic of faith necessitates. It should not escape our minds that the intellect is a power that emotions may exploit before reaching the state of total surrender unto God.

If we seek unity outside ourselves, we will be lost in theories. The topic of unity is always a matter of opposing points of view and insoluble disagreements. It can be seen through various angles. Each one has his own perspective that he believes as true but it is certainly not so to others.

Unity is by no means a matter that can be examined theoretically. Unity is essentially of a divine nature. It is truth and the divine truth has neither angles nor "shifting shadow" (Jam. 1:17). Therefore, due to its simplicity, it is always seen by everyone as a whole at once. It cannot be seen outside or apart from God. This is because he who sees God's attributes necessarily sees God: "He who has seen me has seen the Father" (John 14:10). God said, "I will make all My goodness pass before you" (Ex. 33:19), yet it was said that Moses saw God "face to face" (Ex. 32:11), even though He only saw the goodness of God.

God inhabits and is seen in the heart, so that the heart is filled with God's attributes and comprehends unity in its depth and reality. Unity is a desire of God that Christ

CHRISTIAN UNITY

revealed: "That they may be one in us" (John 17:21). Therefore, unity is to be sought and examined in our heart, if Christ truly is in one's heart. Accordingly, St. Paul prays: "That Christ may dwell in your hearts through faith" (Eph. 3:17).

Unity is now researched in all fields as a prelude to seeking the unity of all in God. This is an illusion. Unity cannot be temporarily separated from God and be used as a means of access to God. Unity can only be a concrete fact when all are in God.

The method used for seeking unity today relies upon rationality, which is exposed to the ebb and flow of emotions. This is a "spiritualized" method of scientific research. However, unity is not a science, and neither is it subject to epistemology based upon the distinction of correct and incorrect, good and evil. Unity is truth, and truth is acquired by inspiration, and the inspiration inhabits the heart first, then the mind. "Did not our heart burn within us while He talked with us... their eyes were opened and they knew Him" (Luke 24:32, 31). This order appears more vividly in the Epistle to the Hebrews, which says:

> This is the covenant that I will make with them after those days, says the Lord: I will put My laws into their hearts, and in their minds I will write them (Heb. 10:16).

Inspiration never neglects reason, but reason always neglects inspiration. We do not wish to neglect seeking unity through the intellect, for the mind reveals the human failings and refutes them. This is the effort and competence of the mind based on analysis that profits a little (Cf. 1 Tim. 4:8

bodily exercise profits a little). On the other hand, the work of unity is essentially a work that edifies the soul and gathers its strengths, which is the competence of the spirit. The spirit pardons, forgives, loves, and unites. Unity rises above the capabilities of the mind. All that the mind is able to do is to understand unity when it is accomplished. However, it does not comprehend how unity will occur before its accomplishment, for it is written, "The kingdom of God does not come with observation" (Luke 17:20).

The gathering of people in this city on one side of the world then in another on the other side of the world is a good practice. For indeed, it is in itself a true preparation for the dwelling of the divine presence, if the meeting is based on the individual willingness of receiving the divine presence, rather than a mere gathering together of the community.

If we desire true unity, we ought to seek it and search for it in God and His presence and not as a theoretical subject separate from God, no matter what theological shape it might take.

In the divine presence, the intellect works as a responder and not as the initiator. This response ought to come from the most powerful activities of the heart. This response echoes the inspiration that accompanies the divine presence.

Unity is to be examined and discerned through the heart through and within the divine presence. Unity apart from the divine presence is nothing more than a mere idea, a matter of discussion or a vain longing.

However, in the presence of God, unity is not only factual and visible but also overwhelming and lived by many. When Christ becomes present amidst the debating community then the debate must cease—each one ought to fill his or her eyes and heart with the true unity and prepare the whole of their inner being to receive and accord that unity.

Any question about unity that is posed on the objective theological plane and remains without a solution is in itself sufficient evidence that the Lord is not present amidst the community. This absence of the Lord proves with certainty that the scope of the meeting, the research methods, and the intention of those gathered ought to be re-examined.

Indeed, if we lift the individual ego and the ecclesial ego from our conscious and subconscious, unity will definitely come to reality. Yet, no individual, no matter how great his control over himself may be, can abandon the ecclesial ego with all its traditional, dialectical, canonical, and sacred traits. Even if we are the representatives of our churches, we cannot give up the ego of our churches. But in the real and true presence of the Lord, all the independent entities that we have created will vanish, and only Christ will become 'the I of all.'

Here, we are not conceding to each other, nor are the churches compromising with each other. Each will present one another to God as everything will be subject to Him at the end of days:

> Now when all things are made subject to Him, then the Son Himself will also be subject to Him who put all things under Him, that God may be all in all (1 Cor. 15:20).

The matter of unity decisively and sharply concerns the presence of the Lord. Through this presence, in fact, unity will divinely take place, and distinctions will be removed. The Lord alone can make "the two into one" and "break down the middle wall of separation" (Eph. 2:14).

CHRISTIAN UNITY

The case is twofold: first, unity and removing of distinctions on the level of "love the Lord, your God," and second, "love your neighbor."

Human logic dictates that the distinctions be removed first for unity to take place. As expressed through divine inspiration (cf. Eph. 2:14), God's logic requires that unity should be accomplished first, so the middle wall of separation would be broken down.

Now this paradox is present in the meetings for Christian unity. The necessity forces itself for us to re-examine the form of the case of unity so it can be according to God.

SECOND: UNITY BASED ON THE INCLINATION TOWARDS COALITION

Unity is the union of one into another to put an end to multiplicity. In outward appearance, unity seems to be a form of weakness. But in its essence, it is an eminent force that is indivisible like God. In contrast, a coalition is the joining of one to another to create multiplicity. In its outward appearance, it seems to be a tendency toward strength and domination, but in its essence it is an unparalleled weakness possessing impotence and fear.

Christian unity is endangered if it is motivated by the instinct of forming a coalition, whether it stems from the weak in order to gain strength or from the powerful to increase their power. In either case, it is a rushing upon the pursuit of earthly life. Living a Christian life would be incompatible with this behavior. "Do not fear those who kill the body" (Matt. 10:28). Strength in the Christian life is derived neither from multiplicity nor from coalition but

CHRISTIAN UNITY

rather from union with God. "For it is God who works in you both to will and to do for His good pleasure" (Phil. 2:13).

To propose unity for a fragile Church that faces oppression, persecution, or poverty is to subject her to a dangerous trial. It subconsciously arouses in her the instinct of coalition to face the danger which anguishes her. This makes the ability of the Church to distinguish between divine unity, which God seeks, and the coalition of multitude, which the instinct of survival seeks, an extremely daunting task.

Therefore, the proposal of Christian unity to a Church facing hostility puts her conscience on trial in a significantly harsher manner than her experience of persecution.

A Church—oppressed by persecution—that chooses Christian unity freely and not just as an escape from a bitter present, is a matter that requires enlightened vision, prudence, mortification, and full submission to God. All of this would still not be enough, as it is necessary for that Church to willfully accept her current bitter state before she considers the possibility of unity. Moreover she should be prepared to joyfully continue on such path of suffering, even to the last member of her congregants. At this point, the longing for unity and its motivations would indeed stem from her divine being and proceed to her from God Himself through His inspiration, rather than instigated by the bitter circumstances or being dictated by instinctive opposition to hostile forces that the Church finds herself in.

To ensure that the weak and persecuted churches comprehend the true meaning of Christian unity, considering her development throughout the history and her modern clashes, and to arouse in her the divine conscience,

CHRISTIAN UNITY

they must first and foremost understand that Christian unity is a state of 'divine weakness' (cf. 1 Cor. 1:25) vis-à-vis the world, similar to the church's Master, who gave up His infinite power to be crucified by whoever wants and in whatever way he wishes. Wishing to manifest the power of His weakness, if appropriate to say so, Christ alerted the disciples, at the time of His tribulations and under the most difficult situations that no defenseless man could endure, by saying: "Do you think that I cannot now pray to My Father, and He will provide Me with more than twelve legions of angels?" (Matt. 26:53).

What prevented the Lord from having an escort like this? How could He be crucified while surrounded by twelve legions of angels? Was this possible?

There is a concealed human danger lurking behind the escort of Christian unity that threatens 'her weakness'—if one may put it in this way. The unity between churches may deceive the sick conscience in that it will secure to the Christians a state of temporal power, even though the Church's temporal 'weakness' is the most precious thing within her since it is her pride and strength, for it is a 'divine weakness,' or as St. Paul says, "the weakness of God is stronger than men" (1 Cor. 1:25).

The Church that possesses temporal power cannot taste a crucifixion forced upon her, for we are not crucified except out of weakness, like the Lord of all who "was crucified in weakness" (2 Cor. 13:4).

When faced with the proposals for Christian unity, the churches, which are considered powerful in a 'temporal' sense or supported by the powers of this age, can fall into a complex of superiority, or putting on the garb of a savior.

CHRISTIAN UNITY

Pilate thought like this when he was seated on the elevated judgement seat while the Lord was tied before him with a chain in the garment of mockery. Pilate said, "Are You not speaking to me? Do You not know that I have power to crucify You, and power to release You?" (John 19:10).

For one to descend from the cross does not prove that he is the Son of God. And he who thinks he can cause another to descend from the cross proves with no doubt that he does not understand the will of the Father.

Temporal weakness goes hand in hand with the cross. In our life, the cross represents a cornerstone. "The cross is the power of God" (1 Cor. 1:18) which is "made perfect in weakness" (2 Cor. 12:9). We demand weakness willingly and endure it when it befalls us with no fear, for, with weakness, there is always grace. "My grace is sufficient for you, for My strength is made perfect in weakness" (2 Cor. 12:9).

Before the cross, the Lord Himself stifled, in both a willing and unwilling manner, the instinct of forming a coalition: "Then all the disciples forsook Him and fled" (Matt. 26:65) and "Therefore, if you seek Me, let these go their way" (John 18:8).

The Lord mocked power when He said to His disciples, "Sell your garment and buy a sword" (Luke 22:36). Worldly power strips us of the power of the Spirit. You either put on Christ, or you put on the world.

When Peter insisted on carrying the sword and used force, he was stripped of grace. Then he denied with his mouth the One he wanted to protect with his sword. This is because when Peter carried the sword and was girded with the intention of murdering, the Spirit abandoned him. Immediately, Satan came and stabbed him with the sword of denial and blasphemy. Thus, the Lord's words were fulfilled, "All who take the sword will perish by the sword" (Matt. 26:52). The Lord here only means spiritual perishing, of which the Lord previously said to Peter, "I have prayed for you that your faith should not fail" (Luke 22:32).

Christian unity loses its divine value the moment it combines with the concept of temporal power, even if its goal is to safeguard the welfare of the weak, and even if it appears to be a beneficial means of mobilizing manpower for pastoral purposes by pressuring the lost sheep. Unity transforms into coalitions doomed to degeneration and extinction, just as all temporal systems created by us are.

We beseech and entreat God for the churches to be united, a unity which is divine in both external appearance and profound essence, a unity beyond time.

ONE CHRIST AND ONE HOLY, CATHOLIC CHURCH

In our sectarian denominationalism-stamped age,[1] when we say, "We believe in one Holy Catholic Church," we tend to think that this oneness refers to our Christian denomination or our doctrine, whether we are Orthodox, Catholic, or Protestant. Consequently, the characteristic of catholicity becomes necessarily associated with the oneness of the denomination.

The Orthodox maintain that the oneness of the Church lies in its orthodoxy and that its catholicity exclusively encompasses all the Orthodox in the world. Such might also be the claim of a Catholic as well as a Protestant. Therefore, the theological understanding of the nature of the Church generally takes shape in every Christian mind, as though the Church's "oneness" were confined within the limits of the doctrine and her "catholicity" were a quality tied up to her locality, which clings to the Church's specific dogma.

In such a narrow-minded understanding that fanatically adheres to modes of thinking and to parochial perspectives, what is lost is the reality of the unlimited nature of the

---

[1] First published in 1972 in the Lebanese review "al-Nūr." Mattā al-Miskīn, "Masīḥ wāḥid wa-kanīsa wāḥida ǧāmiʻa," in *al-Wiḥda al-masīḥiyya fī ḍawʼ maʻnā al-kanīsa wa-ḥaqīqat al-masīḥ* (Wādī al-Naṭrūn: Monastery of Saint Macarius, 2014⁴): 16-23.

Church which transcends human thought as well as its territorial perspective. The Church is greater than us. It is even greater than heaven and earth. For humanity has never filled the Church, nor will we ever be able to do so—even if the whole world, with all its beliefs and systems, were saved, both prospectively and retrospectively—for the only One who can fill the Church is Christ. For He is in Himself the perfect fullness which alone can fill all in all (cf. Eph. 1:23). He is capable to fill us, our mind, time and space.

The universe, with its heaven and earth, cannot contain the Church. Rather, the Church is vast enough to encompass heaven and earth, for the Church is a novel creation—new heaven, new earth, and new humankind. In the essence of such a new infinite creation, the old heaven and earth are swallowed as if they no longer exist—though they actually do. Death is swallowed into life so that it no longer has dominion. The corruptible is swallowed into incorruption so that all is made new, alive, eternal, and pure. The new, in this respect, pertains to the unalterable and infinite whole. The old is what will inevitably perish little by little due to its mutable nature.

Therefore, in her catholicity, the Church is greater than us, all our thoughts, structures, and doctrines. It is even greater than the universe with its immense heavens, the vast earth with all its corruption, and all historical events from their beginning to end.

The Church is the new whole. The character of 'wholeness,' in this respect, for the Church, is derived from the nature of Christ, out of which the Church is formed, and includes all that pertains to humanity and all that pertains to God 'through the Incarnation.' The Church, then, is

ONE CHRIST AND ONE HOLY, CATHOLIC CHURCH

"whole," that is "catholic," for it gathers in the body of Christ, who fills her, all that belongs to humanity and all that belongs to God together into one single entity which is both visible and invisible, finite and infinite, present in the sphere of time and space, but at the same time eternal and metaphysical.

In its Greek root, the word "catholic" is composed by two parts: first, *kath'*, from *katá*, which means 'according,' and second, *ólon* which means 'wholeness.' This wholeness means, here, that which transcends the limited existence. It is an unalterable, infinite, and undivided wholeness. It is an unchangeable wholeness analogous to Christ's nature, without division, confusion or alteration.[2]

Such is the Church, similar in everything to Christ. As Christ is one in His person, comprehensive by His nature, embracing all in His being which is both temporal and eternal, localized and transcending space, so is the 'one catholic' Church. This means that all who are in the Church are necessarily one. And also, they are inevitably one because of her catholicity, i.e., her divine power, which has been delivered to her by Christ to unite every human in God. He who is in Christ is from God and is one in God.

The Church practices her catholicity through her sacraments. Through them, all the believers are brought into unity with the mystical body of Christ, thus becoming all one body and one spirit. This means that they enter into the "One Catholic" nature of the Church. The body of Christ in

---

[2] *The Divine Liturgies of Saints Basil, Gregory and Cyril* (Los Angeles, 2001): 199.

the Church is the mystery of her catholicity and His person is the mystery of her oneness.

Therefore, if the believers in the Church do not attain oneness of heart and mind through the effectiveness of partaking in the one body, and the unity of love through the efficacy of the person of Christ who reigns over all, then the sacraments become no more than mere formality. This is what leads to intellectual and dogmatic disagreement.

The mere formalism of sacraments and dogmas is at odds with the nature of the One omni-comprehensive body, that which whoever eats shall live by it and become one in it, for the source of life and unification of the Church is the body of Christ. For that very body is alive and life-giving and possesses the power to remove the barriers created by time, place, and human speculation and passions, whether they be social, cultural and sociological, or gendered classes, according to St. Paul's words, "Neither *slave nor free* in Christ, neither *Jew nor Greek, barbarian or Scythian*, neither *male nor female*," Gal. 3:28.

The mystical body of Christ in the Church is the source of her power by which she gathers and unites all things in her own self, in her 'One catholic' nature. The Church is the new creation. Adam was the head of the old human creation and the only one from whom all ethnicities, peoples, tribes, and classes emerged. Likewise, Christ became the second Adam, the head of the new human creation and the only one out of whom came forth the new humanity, as the one chosen generation—which is the divine generation of Christ—, along with the one justified people that is gathered by the righteousness of Christ rather than its own self-righteousness, and one holy nation whose only mother is holy baptism rather than the womb of a woman (cf. 1 Pet. 2:9).

The great mystery of Christ's ability to unite peoples and ethnicities on the earth and remove all barriers between them lies behind his being the Incarnate God, the Son of God, and the Son of man simultaneously. The divinity of Christ elevated His humanity above all forms of racism, sexism, and partisanship, and even above sin and death. The sonship of Christ to God made Him gather all of humanity into one sonship to God. Therefore, when we eat the body of Christ, we have all distinctions, sins, and death dissolved within us. We become one with all people, a new and pure creation on the image of Christ, and thus sons of God in the one sonship of Christ. Thus, the "catholic" nature of the Church is dependent on the divine body of Christ as a power that gathers humanity and unifies it all in one sonship to God.

The catholicity of the Church means the catholicity of Christ Himself. It is the efficacy of Christ's nature that is able to bring together God with humanity and humanity within itself at the same time. In other words, given the catholic nature of the Church, she is against all divisions, rifts, and isolations, even all that might cause division or call for it, whatever its source may be internal or external of us.

Christ does not only assemble the scattered ethnicities and peoples in one mind and one faith but also in one body in the full sense of the word with all intimacy, understanding, and love that the one body entails. Hence, the Church, Christ's mystical body, with her Baptism and Eucharist, has become the meeting point of all humanity and the only meeting place for all peoples, ethnicities, and tongues. In her, all distinctions and disagreements dissolve in order that all may become one great and pure body; one spirit, with intimacy and love; one humanity reconciled within itself whose head is Christ. Such creation has all that belongs to peoples, ethnicities, and tongues, including all their features and gifts, without divisions, disputes, or discriminations. This is precisely what "catholicity" means for the Church.

Why has the Church not accomplished her catholicity yet? Or, in other words, why does the Church not live in the world now according to her "catholic" nature, which should be the heart of her life in Christ, the proof of her strength, and the mystery of her perfection and divine wholeness? The answer is straightforward and simple. The Church has yet to attain a pure conscience of her divine realities that transcend the depths of human logic and thought. In other words, the Church still submits the conscience of her divine realities to linguistic and philosophical interpretations, which hinder her to clearly perceive the catholic nature of Christ, which has an extraordinary power to fully reconcile and unify whatever is different—not only thoughts, principles, or doctrines—in a manner beyond the capacity of anyone. This reconciliation is based upon the forgiveness, purification, and justification and even sanctification of everyone by the blood of Christ, with its capacity to forgive the sins of the whole world. It is as if the Church has not yet discovered how deep the power of Christ's blood is, how powerful the action of His body, and the abyss of His love and righteousness.

It is quite evident that almost all of the theological terms which have caused dogmatic schisms are not defective in themselves. Rather, the defect is a result of their interpretations and understandings. This is due to us approaching the divine—meaning God's simple and pure nature—with the mind of Adam and his understanding, and not with the mind of Christ. Therefore, the schism was inevitable and a necessity dictated by the nature of the sons of Adam that are divided against themselves.

Schism has no place in Christ's mind and understanding, neither has it any reality in His person or in His "catholic" nature. Rather, schism occurred due to the existing division within human nature, which has been distorted with sin. Thus, human nature became full of hatred, doubts, suspicions, pride, and divisions. As a result, division is not in the Church's nature but rather in the distorted understanding and perception of the truth of Christ and the Church.

Hence, we can see that if we introduce any division into the very nature of Christ and the Church, it means that we have used a non-theological, fallen, human approach to the divine. Every schism which occurred in the Church resulted from our attempt to solve ecclesial matters with an ethnocentric mind, which divides, that is to say, with a non-ecclesial and non-Catholic thought.

Therefore, only the 'new' humanity, which has the mind of Christ, sees Christ as one with no possibility of division, conflict, or disagreement within Himself. The Church will remain unique in the whole world only when the "new" humanity fully receives the nature of Christ in its depths. She is at the same time one and catholic, that is she gathers all people, and orthodox in all thought with no sectarianisms, denominationalisms, or schisms within herself.

When people deny their own wills, then and only then, the one will of Christ becomes visible. When people give up their passions and hatred and submit their bodies and minds to the action of the Holy Spirit, then and then only, the mystical body of Christ is manifested and exerts His work in the Church in unifying all the hearts, principles, and thoughts. When people sincerely surrender their lives to Christ, then and only then, the life of Christ becomes visible in the Church, and His Spirit is poured all over the world.

If every soul within the Church spiritually, faithfully, and sincerely submits to God in fervent repentance, and if every Church submits herself to God in the same manner, only then, by the grace of God, will the Church become one. The churches will be united by the power of the Holy Spirit and Christ will become the one Shepherd for the one flock, ruling the Church Himself with His Spirit, and thus becoming the source of her catholicity and unity.

Is not the Church the manifestation of Christ's incarnation on earth and the continuity of His incarnation in time? Is it not in the Church that the believers form the new human nature, glorified in the person of Christ and adopted through Him to God? How can Christ be revealed in the Church except through the unity of mind and will, and through the awareness of the human and spiritual oneness of the sons of the one God, "who are born not of blood, nor of the will of the flesh, nor of the human will, but of God?" (John 1:13).

How can it be proven to the world that God is one if not through the unity of those born of Him?

How can the world be certain that Jesus Christ is God's only begotten Son except through the oneness of the sonship of those who believe in Him, whom He has born unto God by dying for them and resurrecting them by His resurrection, who are now united to His body, blood, and spirit, thus becoming all members of one body?

Is it not quite evident from the foregoing that the whole theology is in the catholicity and the unity of the Church? Do they not reveal Christ's existence and work? Are they not the fulfillment of our new birth which has been granted to us from heaven, through water and Spirit?

The inadequacies observed in different churches concerning the catholicity and unity of the Church ought not to prompt any of us to reevaluate our theological stance. — for our theology is truthful and faithful—but rather reexamine ourselves in view of our sound theology that we may rectify our perception of God as one Father unto all people and our understanding of Christ as one Savior and Redeemer to all who call upon His name. He is the One who adopted all of humanity unto God without partiality. We ought to reconsider our love for fellow human beings. — every human being—considering them indisputably brothers and sisters unto us, even if he or she considers us enemies and sets for us the traps of death.

Therefore, we ought to fully comprehend that what moves us to this ecclesial catholicity and Church unity is not a mere theological zeal, sublime principles, or even remorse. Rather, it should stem from our faith and love, that is to say, the reality of the newness of life we live, and from our heavenly birth, which cannot be turned into a living reality apart from the catholicity and unity of the Church.

The new man (cf. Eph. 2:15) cannot live in isolation apart from one another, or divided from one another, or from a spot of hatred and animosity toward one other. The new man ought to be "whole" and ought to be "one," for he possesses a universal nature and emerges from only one Father. The one new nature with which everyone is born into the Church causes "all to become one" through grace and Spirit. In this very process, God's love imposes its divine unifying authority on the one hand, and, on the other, His one paternity marks all who are born of the Father with the image of Christ, His Only-begotten Son.

The Church is *Catholic* for she is the *body* of the Son given for the whole world by love (cf. John 3:16) who recapitulates all things in Himself (cf. Eph. 1:10). The Church is *one*, for she is the house of the Father which cannot ever be divided against herself. Now, with great yearning, tears, prayers, and the consciousness of the new man, we look forward to the fulfillment of the catholicity and unity of the Church in the whole world.

TRUE UNITY WILL BE AN INSPIRATION FOR THE WORLD

Doctrines are Untouchable

Doctrines regarding a church signifies her existence.[1] For instance, from the very moment the Coptic orthodox doctrines came into existence, the Coptic Orthodox Church came into existence. Given that the doctrines still exist as they are, the Coptic Church is still manifestly present as well. Doctrine is not a mere list of articles of faiths, statements, or canons. Rather, it is above all a spiritual worship and a living faith with clear and distinct features. These distinct features give each doctrine its own character so that, as much as the doctrine clings to this specific character, it will live and flourish. Otherwise, the doctrine will alter its form and name, perhaps even cease to exist.

The survival of the distinct features of doctrines throughout the ages did not happen through memorization, faithful recording, or apologetic production. Rather, it was out of love, attachment, and living practice of those doctrines. Additionally, it was out of efforts to interpret, contemplate, and define them, through the discovery of the truth hidden within. This living and rich heritage was

---

[1] First published in 1984. Mattā al-Miskīn, *al-Wiḥda al-ḥaqīqiyya satakūn ilhāman li-l-ʿālam* (Wādī al-Naṭrūn: Monastery of Saint Macarius, 2012⁶).

TRUE UNITY WILL BE AN INSPIRATION...

handed down by the generations through living tradition, which was then recorded. In this manner, the Church, together with her doctrine, has survived. The doctrines were compiled with great care with precise explanations, definitions, and codifications through the various generations. As a result, the history of any church became the history of her doctrines. Also, the history of a church's hierarchs and prominent teachers became the history of the extent of their adhering to or their forsaking of her doctrines. Doctrines regarding a church assumed a canonical framework that cannot be touched or neglected because it dictates her very essence, which explains her existence, history, love, and spirit.

Likewise, Christianity, or rather Christ, has taken a home in every culture, assuming its features and giving it His life in return. Christ looks like He is dark-skinned in Africa, blonde in the Northern countries, of darker skin in India, and of a shorter height in the far North at the Inuit. To all of those, He is the One Christ Himself, Christ of Golgotha, of the tomb and the resurrection, Christ of the whole world.

Therefore, it is pointless that the various churches, in their zeal for Christian unity, attempt to change the dogmatic expressions of any Church either by adding or by omitting parts of them. Otherwise, we would be like one who wants to flay an African person's dark skin or dye the skin of a European person. This attempt is like wiping out a person's identity,[2] or better, trying to create a version of Christ without humanity!

---

[2] The author uses skin color and stature as representative of the profundity of thought, emotion, and philosophy that are manifest

TRUE UNITY WILL BE AN INSPIRATION...

Does this mean we should abandon Christian unity? God forbid. Christian unity is the ultimate quest of faith to the extent that it overflows in our being and causes our hearts and emotions to vibrate. Therefore, we seek unity with tears, for we seek Christ. We desire to live it in spirit and truth because we want to taste Christ, to live His love, and to enjoy the mystery of His unity with the Father. This unity is the essence of divine love. Christ Himself urges us to seek such unity, teaching us:

> I do not pray for these alone, but also for those who will believe in Me through their word; that they all may be one, as You, Father, are in Me, and I in You; that they also may be one in Us, that the world may believe that You sent Me... I in them, and You in Me; that they may be made perfect in one, and that the world may know that You have sent Me, and have loved them as You have loved Me. And I have declared to them Your name, and will declare it, that the love with which You loved Me may be in them, and I in them (John 17:20-21, 23, 26).

We ought to turn with a real understanding toward the depth of this prayer. Christ here does not plead for the unity of the letter but rather of the Spirit, not the unity of thought and view but the unity of love. The prayer does not limit itself to our unity in understanding who Christ is, but rather aims toward our unity in Him. This does not come through our gathering in the presence of Christ (outside of us) in the form of an assembly for an intellectual reconciliation.

---

in the distinctive features of the natural, intellectual, and spiritual heritage of all the world's ethnic groups.

Rather, it comes only through "the love... may be in them, and I in them" (John 17:26).

Does this mean we should stop prayer meetings, ecumenical assemblies, and dialogues in addition to ceasing to present proposals and studies aiming to bring the various views closer to one another? May it never be! Rather, the crucial question is: with which one should we start? The letter or the spirit? Canons or life? Contents of the faith and doctrine or their essence?

It is wise to bear in mind that commencing meetings with the letter will kill the spirit and ultimately result in lists of terminologies and formulas. If we starting with the canons, we may perceive ourselves as consistently correct and in possession of the definitive truth, while the other side appears to be always wrong. We get trapped in this axis of thought, going in circles, until time—and with it, life—will slip away from us. If we start with the contents of the doctrine, we will never be able to reach its essence. On the contrary, it is the Spirit who has produced the letter. He is the only One who can complete it and give it life. Life in Christ comes first. It is His life who embraces the human mind to produce a frame for faith. Life in Christ is the only thing that possesses the ability to make the rigidity of the canons flexible to contain more of life and be more embracing. Finally, it is the essence of the doctrine that must be pursued because it is Christ Himself that no content will limit.

Exiting the Rigidness of Division

Therefore, it is necessary that the theological dialogue starts with the spirit rather than the letter. First by receiving

TRUE UNITY WILL BE AN INSPIRATION...

in us the life of the One Christ, before reconciling the articles of the dogma with their various formulations. We ought to live the only essence of the doctrine together before we agree on the contents. The essence of doctrine—that is to say Christ Himself—is based on love, sacrifice, redemption, and total abnegation even to the form of a servant. In this manner, the dialogue of the heart with the conscience will arrive at astonishing results that are truthful, as they will proclaim the voice of Christ Himself.

This occurs over three steps. First, churches should lift simultaneously the anathemas against each other, for they are against the will of the Holy Spirit. Anathemas were the result of each Church's ignorance of the spirit and conscience of the other Church and the clinging to the letter rather than to the spirit. The reciprocal anathematization is the main hurdle that came in the way of all the attempts of unity in previous gatherings and dialogue sessions. For how can there be an agreement on formulas of reconciliation and unity while each Church is still excommunicated by the other?[3]

---

[3] This booklet was published in 1984 and thus this recommendation preceded by six years the official statement made in the *Second Agreed Statement and Recommendations to the Churches* at the end of the dialogue session between the Orthodox and the Oriental Orthodox churches in Chambésy (Switzerland) in 1990. "Both families agree that all the anathemas and condemnations of the past which now divide us should be lifted by the churches in order that the last obstacle to the full unity and communion of our two families can be removed by the grace and power of God. Both families agree that the lifting of anathemas and condemnations will be consummated on the basis that the councils and the fathers previously anathematized or condemned are not heretical" (Cf.

TRUE UNITY WILL BE AN INSPIRATION...

The second step is the reciprocal and concurrent recognition between the Chalcedonians and non-Chalcedonians of the doctrine of one another. This recognition must be based on the essence rather than the literal content of the formulation, and on the basis of the mystery of salvation and eternal life, which both theological systems offer through Jesus Christ who works in the same way in both, despite the difference of formulations.

Lastly, beginning a discussion on the contents of the doctrines, and removing ambiguities by explanation. There should not be omissions or additions to the doctrinal points, handed down through tradition to each Church. Such a discussion aims to offer a reconciliatory formulation that suits the unity of the communion and the spirit, without compromising the things pertaining to the history of the doctrines, their subcategories, the various writings, and councils concerning them. This means a reciprocal and concurrent confession between the Orthodox sides in dialogue that the doctrine of each side is sound, as well as an acceptance of their communion in Christ. Rather, we ought to accept Christ Himself in our communion and commune of one chalice. This should not be based on the letter of the dogmas, but rather on the basis of the living Christ dwelling in the heart of each Church and on the Holy Spirit who is at work and active for our salvation in the Church. Only then should we begin the dialogue of formulations and clauses, without touching the heritage of each Church, with its spiritual tradition, its

---

Meyer, H. et alii. *Growth in Agreement II: Reports and Agreed Statements of Ecumenical Conversations on a World Level, 1982-1998* (Geneva: WCC Publications, 2000): 196).

theological understanding, and whatever has derived from it, whether in writings or councils.

In this manner, as we are united in spirit in God's love and the communion of the Holy Spirit, the One Christ will oblige us, or rather inspire us, to acquire one mind, one word, and one utterance. Each Church will not lose her theological formulations and distinct characteristics which are the very same characteristics of the One Christ who lives in her. As per the analogy we presented earlier, the one communion will occur through the Spirit in the one faith without the dark-skinned person being asked to flay himself, nor by asking the white-skinned individual to dye his skin. Christ in the world has made the North and the South His homeland. He has taken the features of all, so that He has become "white and ruddy" and "dark and lovely" (Song of Songs 5:10; 1:5).

The Church and the World

The Church knows no bounds when she engages with the world. The Church's spiritual labor encompasses the entire world as its mission field. This includes engaging with the various conflicting ideologies—both positive and negative—that exist globally, and the world's diverse affairs, politics, and governments. As we read in the Gospel, "go into all the world" (Mark 16:15), "in all nations" (Mark 13:10, Matt. 28:19), that is to say that, every human being, or in other words humanity itself, regardless of thoughts and morals, is the object of the Church's solicitude. The Church's work in the world consists of her life in Christ, her joy in Him, and her experience with Him. Her work is manifested firstly in a holy life that acts as a leading role model. Then, it is offered

TRUE UNITY WILL BE AN INSPIRATION...

in words of sincere and inspired love and joyful acts of consolation for others, turning the hearts of fathers to their sons and sons to their fathers (cf. Luke 1:17), subduing the mind and heart of humanity to abundant life (cf. John 10:10).

Christ did not come to a certain church with a limited place within a specific building, with a certain name, or a specific environment, or to a particular people, with an exacting mindset or heritage. He is neither bound to the tabernacle nor the temple, as in the old times. Rather, His Father sent Him to the world which He loved, to the whole creation that became His temple with no boundaries: "For the temple of God is holy, which temple you are" (1 Cor. 3:17).

In its alienation from God, the world has never starved for truth, justice, peace, and love as much as it does today. So much so, that it has become enslaved to so many opinions and trends. Within the Church is the Bread of Life for the world. The Church is Bethlehem for all the nations. Christ has entrusted her with the basket of the seven loaves, which still possesses the mystery of filling the four thousand, or even millions (cf. Mark 8:1-9). This starvation is not for bread so much as it is for the word of truth, love and life. However, it is not a sincere hunger for God that people feel, like they did in the old times. Rather, it is a hunger concealed behind rebellion. The human soul is in uttermost need of God. However, the soul has turned away from Him, due to various factors. The most critical of them are the carelessness of the Church, the bad state of the pasture, and the ignorance of the shepherds. Today, Christ's parable is fulfilled: the sheep flee the hireling and are instead handed to the wolf with the task of shepherding them (cf. John 10:12). Unless the Bread of Life

TRUE UNITY WILL BE AN INSPIRATION...

is kneaded with the sweat of godliness and baked with the fire of trials and with real experience, it is abhorred by souls.

In ancient times, the menorah in the temple used to indicate God's presence amidst the people to enlighten their minds amid the ignorance of the pagan world. In our time, the Church is that very light that is able to dispel the darkness of human ignorance throughout the world—God has entrusted this light to the world in order to illuminate the path of life and immortality before everyone. No darkness will stand against this light, no matter how much darkness dominates a person, a community, a congregation, or a country unless the Church turns from her light and resides in the shadow.

Darkness now is battling against the light. The light, broken, is shrinking before it. The lamp of God is barely lit in the hands of the preachers and the teachers. The light of the Church no longer derives its oil from the stores of godliness and grace which pour in the heart of those who witness with words ringing out as if they were from the mouth of God: "As from God, we speak in the sight of God" (2 Cor. 2:17). Such words are capable of dispersing the distorted thoughts burdened with the surfeit of intellectualism and technologism, which have corrupted the simplicity of life from the Spirit in Christ. Hence, the power of eloquent words alone is no longer sufficient to move the hearts of people. Rather, the words are in a dire need for the "demonstration of the Spirit and power" (1 Cor. 2:4) so that the preacher can deliver the person of the living Christ, crucified and redeemer, who is able to fill the void of the heart, mind, and soul with all the joys of the Spirit, so that every soul may taste and be filled by the closeness to the Father in the fullness of the Spirit and the holiness of Christ.

In the book of Revelation, not everyone can say to others "come," but rather, "let him who hears say, 'Come!'" (Rev. 17:22). A preacher cannot self-promote, or else the word would cease from his mouth, "For we do not preach ourselves, but Christ Jesus the Lord, and ourselves your bondservants for Jesus' sake" (2 Cor. 4:5). When will the Church put herself in the place of the slave unto the congregation? I mean the slave, not the hired servant, who has rights and a wage. On the contrary, the slave has duties and no rights. He serves faithfully, expecting no reward for his service or his faithfulness. It is sufficient for him to remain joyful in his master's house, fully ready to lay down his life for the sake of his master and the children of his master. In this very same manner, the Church was and is founded on the blood of the martyrs: "For Your sake we are killed all day long" (Rom. 8:36), rather than on mere words.

The Church in the Gospel and the mind of Christ is a bride. If the bride undervalues her purity and does not sanctify herself—as presented in all those who carry her name and garment—then who will desire purity, or who will be able to attain holiness or come to the bridegroom? Who can blame those who entered and left regretful?

In the book of Revelation, the Church is portrayed as a spring of living water like her Teacher, according to the Spirit which is within her:

> And the Spirit and the bride say, 'Come!' And let him who hears say, 'Come!' And let him who thirsts come. Whoever desires, let him take the water of life freely (Rev. 22:17).

TRUE UNITY WILL BE AN INSPIRATION...

What should we proclaim if the spring of the Spirit, love, and godliness dries within the Church? Even if she were to proclaim, who would listen or attend to take in her words? What will become of those who are thirsty for righteousness? Should they stray from the path and seek solace and joy from the devil's springs, who ought to be blamed but the Church? The world is filled with unending sciences, know-hows, and ideologies. However, only one spring that leads to life eternal is entrusted to the Church by God.

In the timeless parables of Christ regarding the kingdom, the Church is presented as the unique pearl which a wise merchant found it so precious that he sold all that he had and bought it (cf. Matt. 13:45-46). This pearl became unto him a source of richness that remains beyond the end of time. In the book of Revelation, the pearl is the door leading to the heavenly Jerusalem (cf. Rev. 21:21). In the teachings of Christ, it is evident that He is the very door that leads to eternal life.

However, if the Church gets corrupted in her mind and deviates away from the simplicity which is in Christ, can she still be considered a pearl? If the crafty serpent, which once deceived Eve, deceives her by turning her heart toward the glory, the power, the money, the various businesses, and the lust over the powers of this age, can she still be considered a pearl? Would it still be possible to know the way that leads to the door or the password for passing the threshold? If our incapability is revealed, causing everyone to lean toward his or her own way, while opinions and perspectives multiply and deceptions increase, who can apportion blame? And who would correct these ideas, knowing that thought is not corrected by another but, instead, by a life founded on correct thought? Reading the Gospels, displaying verses, and practicing preaching, apart from the mystery of Christ's presence, are mere pious expressions that can be used for the sake of the ego rather than Christ.

Christ has entrusted the Church with the mystery of His body. The Church is either the body of Christ, "the fullness of Him who fills all in all" (Eph. 1:23), or else she is empty with nothing to fill her. The greatest characteristic of the body of Christ is that it is still able to die and rise daily in the Church: "For your sake we face death all day long; we are considered as sheep to be slaughtered" (Rom. 8:36); "Now if we died with Christ, we believe that we will also live with him" (Rom. 6:8). In this death and resurrection, generation after generation lives. The Church that avoids and flees from dying to herself and to the world on the cross loses the gift and the power of the resurrection, which is the victory over the world. In this case, the Church shrinks at the end under the power of the world. Consequently, she loses the capacity to judge the world.

The strongest power concealed in the body of Christ, in the Church, and in us who are "flesh of His flesh and bones of His bones" (cf. Eph. 5:30; Gen. 2:23) is the mystical force of attraction that is wholly hidden within Him at all levels: "And I, if I am lifted up from the earth, will draw all peoples to Myself" (John 12:32). If the Church desires to be at such a level, she ought to serve the mystery of the divine attraction hidden in the body of Christ entrusted within her. That is to say, she ought to gather all in Christ and, for the sake of Christ, to manifest her oneness in all, through the Gospel, sacraments, tradition, and history in order to serve every human stature in the Church and every soul that lives in her bosom. Inasmuch as the Church is lifted from the earth and

TRUE UNITY WILL BE AN INSPIRATION...

the dust within her spirit, thought, and goals the force of the divine attraction is energized, allowing her to lift everyone in the mystery of the cross to fulfill the mystery of the risen body, according to the will of Christ. As for Christ, He has been lifted from the earth through His death, even the death of the cross (cf. Phil. 2:8). Thus, how can the Church be lifted up in order to be able to draw others to Christ except through this very death, whether by free, conscious, and determined will or unwillingly, in weakness, in full submission to Him in whose hands there is death and life? "For though He was crucified in weakness, yet He lives by the power of God" (2 Cor. 13:4). St. Paul discovered the mystery of attraction in this weakness and this very death, as he says, "For to me, to live is Christ, and to die is gain" (Phil. 1:21); "Most gladly I will rather boast in my infirmities, that the power of Christ may rest upon me" (2 Cor. 12:9). Christ founded the Church through His weakness, not through His strength.

The Church's existence and life are founded in the mysteries of the divine attraction hidden in the body of Christ. There is no way other than accepting weakness and death to achieve the perfection of the body of Christ, a perfection that must be in our minds without any borders or denominations whatsoever. If it is so, how can a Church, then, be satisfied or have comfort knowing she is separated from another Church that carries the same body of Christ with His wounds and sufferings, along with His death which He underwent on the cross to draw everyone unto Himself (cf. John 12:32)? And who is referred to by "everyone"? The Chalcedonians or the non-Chalcedonians? The Eastern or the Western? The Northern or the Southern?

TRUE UNITY WILL BE AN INSPIRATION...

A Peaceful Vision of the Schism Between the Chalcedonians and Non-Chalcedonians

In the contemporary Christian world, political and international issues are often analyzed either on the basis of pure ideology or on the basis of the various bloody conflicts that occur between nations and even among citizens of the same country as the inevitable result of competing ideologies. Yet, many fail to recognize that the Church is a major contributor to contemporary atrocities because she has lost her primary role in reconciling the world with God due to her current state of weakness and frailty. This weakness has affected her spirituality and piety, which was once able to let nations live in fear of God and grow in what is good for us according to the intent of God: "Bringing every thought into captivity to the obedience of Christ" (2 Cor. 10:5). Moreover, weakness has so penetrated the depths of her theological thought that the respectful approach toward Scripture has been shaken in all modern theological schools. The fear is no longer of God, but rather for God Himself, lest He lose His dignity and presence in the curriculums of these schools and the hearts of many of their theologians. In this manner, the reverence for the Church has been lost, that same Church which once had the final authoritative word over the world which she used to derive from the power of truth through the Holy Spirit, who strengthens the unity of thought, word, and work. Therefore, the very foundations of the Church have been shaken, though the Church was once seen by the world as "the pillar and ground of the truth" (1 Tim. 3:15).

This division in thought within the churches today comes about from a series of events throughout history that we have

TRUE UNITY WILL BE AN INSPIRATION...

unjustly inherited due to the quarrels and divisions following the council of Chalcedon and its aftermath in the fifth century.

The tragic question that will remain unanswered is: why did the strong and mighty brothers in the Lord and in spirit fall into dispute? How were they driven to enmity? Furthermore, upon whom did God put the hope of reconciling the world to Himself?

Then comes another question even more tragic and painful: how did they all enter the Council of Chalcedon full of hope that they would arrive at the unity of faith, thought, and word, trying to get rid of every thought which is not pleasing God's goodness? How did they leave this council excommunicated, humiliated, slapped on their faces, and with their teeth broken, starting the history of the greatest schism? This schism affected and undermined the strength of the whole Christian world, paralyzing the East, like a spoil for anyone to claim, and leaving the West in pain, unable to provide help or sympathy.

What makes this atrocity more painful and ambiguous is what, in the modern days, the most true-hearted Orthodox theologians have concluded after attending the reconciliation meetings between the Chalcedonians and non-Chalcedonians on the following occasions:

Aarhus in Denmark – August 1964
Bristol in England – July 1967
Geneva in Switzerland – August 1970
Addis Ababa in Ethiopia – January 1971[4]

---

[4] After *True Unity Will be an Inspiration For the World* was published, four other meetings took place: Chambésy

The tragedy here is that they have come to discover together that this dreadful schism that lasted for 1500 years, causing the Christian world to inherit unparalleled weakness, helplessness, and disgrace, had no justification at all.

However, these dialogue sessions were the first step since the schism, which the churches courageously take to move from the despair of division and the atrocity of isolation towards a likeness of reconciliation. With this, a streak of hope began to appear in the sky of the East, proclaiming that the Christian unity is worthy of declaring its spiritual authority once more. This will allow the Church to wipe from her face the wounds of history and soothe the hearts of the saints who have reposed with the hope of the arrival of this day. This will also encourage the weak-hearted of the present generations, who have been victims of individualism and division, suffering from the pains of isolation. And at the end, the reconciliation will please the heart of God.

What are the Benefits which can Proceed from Unity?

1. Practically and spiritually, lifting the anathemas will entail removing the obstacles that impede the Holy Spirit from renewing His work among the churches by pouring new gifts for the welfare of the exhausted world and of each individual church.

(Switzerland), 1985; Anba Bishoy (Egypt), 1989; Chambésy, 1990; Chambésy, 1993 (cf. Gros, J. et alii. *Growth in Agreement III: International Dialogue Texts and Agreed Statements, 1998—2005* (Geneva: WCC Publications, 2007)).

2. Accepting communion from the one chalice would mean making the two parties one through the cross (cf. Eph. 2:14-16), in order to elevate the mystery to its full strength. This means accepting the power of the blood of Christ, which alone has the power to cast out enmity and to perfect the reconciliation in the one body.

3. Accepting the reconciliation means accepting a new power of forgiveness from God as a reward for the act of forgiveness that takes place reciprocally between the churches. This is a matter of quittance of conscience from the debt which was weakening each Church imperceptibly: "For if you forgive men their trespasses, your heavenly Father will also forgive you" (Matt. 6:14).

4. The churches giving up their hostility, which they lived for 1500 years, means essentially communal repentance. This repentance in itself will instill a tremendous power, causing heaven to rejoice and will bring about days of prosperity and peace for the whole world:

> Repent therefore and be converted, that your sins may be blotted out, so that times of refreshing may come from the presence of the Lord, and that He may send Jesus Christ, who was preached to you before, whom heaven must receive until the times of restoration of all things, which God has spoken by the mouth of all His holy prophets since the world began (Acts 3:19-21).

Is it the time for the "restoration of all things" as per the fullness of God's purpose? Would the Son of God find the faith undivided between us, that none of us may be prevented from seeing Him as He is (cf. 1 John 3:2)?

5. If the Orthodox churches are able to overcome the barriers which are standing in the way of fulfilling the unity

TRUE UNITY WILL BE AN INSPIRATION...

of faith, love, and worship among them, then the power of this very reconciliation will be released in the world to sweep away the rest of the barriers which have burdened our hearts and minds, be it churches or individuals.

The first schism among the Orthodox, which took place in Chalcedon in the fifth century, occurred without the Church realizing the grave consequences that would surround the Christian world as a result of it. This first schism paved the way to the second one in the eleventh century between the Catholics and the Orthodox, whose exorbitant price the world continues to pay in terms of weakness, division, and quarrels on all levels. The Church did not comprehend that she is the one who planted the spirit of hostility and division in the world—a spirit that spread among the nations and individuals, which became the approach of the governments and countries. Therefore, having reaped the bitterness of her actions, the Church ought to work in the godliness and love of Christ, carrying the burdens of this divided, devastated world that bent to self-destruction.

However, the Church will neither be able, nor be qualified, nor entrusted by God to pray or care about a divided world while she remains shattered herself. As long as she is divided against herself, she will not be able to provide a solution to the divisions that are in the world but can only bear their burden. The current ecclesial reconciliation is a necessity the world needs and awaits it impatiently, even if the world is not aware of the strength and extent of this unity.

6. Rather than individualism and division, the core of our Orthodox churches (Eastern and Oriental) is unity, which is the natural result of the doctrine of communion. Unity—the fulfillment of communion—occurring among

TRUE UNITY WILL BE AN INSPIRATION...

the Orthodox churches appears to be daunting due to the long division and some political factors that have played a major role in creating the spirit of animosity in the fifth century. However, unity remains the cornerstone of our spiritual, sociological, and even theological essence. An essential element of the Orthodox faith is the affirmation of the faith in the communion of saints. The Church insists that she is a spiritual family, or as St. Paul puts it "members of the household of God" (Eph. 2:19), be it in the life of the individual, the community, the Church or the proclamation of dogma.

Upon closer examination of this spiritual and theological quality, it becomes evident that unity is today lacking in the Western world, where an excessive emphasis is placed on individualism across all spheres—work, family, society, and religion. Should this spirit proliferate, it will have the capacity to obliterate the Church's cohesiveness, thereby diminishing the likelihood of salvation and the spreading of the message of life to those who are lost in the midst of technological advancements and urban sprawl, enslaved to the entertainment industry and mass media, which eradicate any possibility of us ever being a part of a church, community, or even a family. Moreover, they eradicate from us the essence of love, familiarity, and longing for our heavenly home.

If we Orthodox fulfill our unity, then the divine doctrine of unity, i.e., living in the "communion of saints," will be animated within us in its practical form. Consequently, the Church shall revert to its initial spiritual form, resembling the Last Supper in which Christ is surrounded by His disciples. This spirit of unity is in harmony with our own spirit and nature. It is able to nurture the whole community with a new understanding of divine love in its largest extent, in a way in which the passionate love for Christ will not be exclusive to monastics and hermits. Rather, it will be a free gift extended according to the stature of Him who grants it, that it may be given to all who share the same image: "He will make those of one image dwell in one house" (Ps. 68:6 LXX). This house is the Church assembled in an authentic spirit of communion. As she did in her first days, the Orthodox Church will then be capable of universally proclaiming her message immersed in the divine love and passion for Christ.

Therefore, we deduce that the fulfillment of unity among the Orthodox churches will create new forces for evangelizing for the well-being of the world, which estranged itself from God. The Holy Spirit will even use it to pour out upon the world the spirit of watchfulness for a mass conversion and return so that all will seek the face of God: "You said, 'Seek My face' [...] 'Your face, Lord, I will seek'" (Ps. 27:8).

For the benefit of the entire world, this unity could be realized if we were genuinely capable of surrender ourselves to the Holy Spirit's will without erecting barriers in our way before God. The Spirit is awaiting what we will faithfully do for the sake of unity, that He may do a hundred times more. For unity among the churches cannot occur or be achieved apart from the Holy Spirit and His sole will. However, its initial move is contingent upon our desire and free will. The Spirit is awaiting what we will faithfully do for the sake of unity, that He may do a hundred times more. 7.   There is a law in spiritual matters which differs from its counterpart in material matters. In the material world, if we add a to b the result will be $a+b$. In spiritual matters, when we add the spirituality of a group of people or a Church (a) side by side with the spirituality of another group (b) the result will be $a \times b$ and not $a+b$, i.e., it is a multiplication rather than an addition. This causes the end result of $a \times b$, $b \times a$, thus putting these spiritualities to multiply in a mystical and wondrous manner. Each one of the two will have the gifts of the other party united to his or her own gifts as if they were his or her very own.

In this manner, what is truly astonishing is that each Church will be able to gain through her unity with the other Church what allows her to reach a higher stage of progress in spiritual matters that she could never reach on her own. In this mystery lies the new power that derives from the infinite nature of God, which the world needs today and cannot find in any Church, no matter how powerful this Church is. This is because the world will not reach the great power of Christ *except in the full stature of Christ,* that is, in the unity of His body, a body which the Church represents now divided and torn apart because of its divisions.

This unity concealed in the mystery of communion, which is crippled by the current divisions, represents indeed the power of transfiguration the world has been laboring for with the bitterness of deadly pain, for the world awaits its new birth: "The kingdoms of this world have become the kingdoms of our Lord and of His Christ" (Rev. 11:15). Therefore, the mystery of great unity is the mystery of transfiguration and the mystery of infinity encompassed in the one body of Christ. This mystery is not accomplished except in the unity of communion. It is the only power by which the world can be transfigured, with God's presence saving it from destruction. Therefore, it is necessary for the churches to derive from this truth a power that can free her from her rigidity, selfishness, individualism, and sometimes cowardliness, to be able to embrace all the demands of unity.

8. It is evident that the world is constantly moving toward being freed from the Church, for the Church is always giving it the chance to be freed from her, inasmuch as the Church frees herself from total submission and intimacy with God. Therefore, the return of the world to the spirit of the Church depends upon the Church's return to the Spirit of God. The Christian world, without a doubt, cannot be united to God apart from the Church. In the Church, the righteousness of God is revealed through faith in Christ for repentance, salvation, and intimacy with God.

Everyone who has experienced genuine repentance and been revealed the mystery of salvation is aware that the world does not revolve around itself, but rather expands through time. The rate at which the world is transforming is astounding, and those who live the mystery of salvation recognize that the world is not moving towards obscurity or nothingness as it turns away from itself. In their depths, the spiritual persons perceive that, despite its bleak path, the world is moving towards God through its failures. Its faltering path is not, however, devoid of inspired individuals, great men and women, and saints, who are now a minority unable to exert influence on the world. The Church is in a state of extreme weakness, unable to inspire the way to God to the world. Does anyone understand this?

The Church—every Church, Chalcedonian or non-Chalcedonian—assumes that she is working for the well-being of her congregation alone. In doing so, she is occupied with herself, unwilling to realize that the well-being of her congregation cannot be compared to the fate of the world.

TRUE UNITY WILL BE AN INSPIRATION...

Disregarding global affairs and people's concerns, every Church that only attends to the needs of her own members consecrates the bitterness of division and devoid the chalice of communion within the Church of the spirit of communion. The presence of Christ in the Church is void of the world which God has loved and redeemed.

9. Christ pleaded:

> I do not pray for these alone, but also for those who will believe in Me through their word; that they all may be one, as You, Father, are in Me, and I in You; that they also may be one in Us, that the world may believe that You sent Me (John 17:20).

The unity Christ seeks for us 'all', is for every person, Church, and all who desire to be included in this plead of His, or who are willing to obey His call, or are receptive to this great commandment of His. This is a mystical unity whose criteria the human mind cannot exhaust and whose limits it cannot imagine. Let us pay attention. Such attempts to subdue unity to the abilities of the human mind would be sufficient for us to miss the mystery of Christ and Christianity, as it is at the level of Christ's being in the Father and the Father's being in Christ. Not only in terms of the eternal Word, but in the sense of the Man Jesus Christ. This is the unity for which God accepted the blood of Christ shed on the cross as its price.

In this perspective the mystery of eternal salvation is concealed with the mighty power of God, which caused the resurrection of Christ. Therefore, it is a power granted to us, the Church, and the world to trample on death and abolish mortality, entering into the newness of life with God, surpassing time and its horrors that threaten human existence.

Christ puts the dimensions of the power of His unity with the Father and the unity of the Father with Him as a pattern for the unity He desires for us in Him and among one another: "That they also may be one in Us" (John 17:21). Because He perceives that this unity exceeds our abilities and expectations, He pleads for it from the Father Himself, and He still pleads for it through His blood.

Therefore, the desired unity of churches is not a unity with geographical or temporal dimensions—as it might be said—neither can it be based on a human or an intellectual foundation, whatever they may be. This is because the unity ought to be a unity with the Father through Christ first. Then, the deeds and power of Christ will be revealed in us on the temporal and spatial level later on. However, Christ had foreknowledge that this unity, which will gather us in Him to the Father, will be endowed with gifts, powers, and transcendent effects on the whole of humanity. This is the reason why He reveals plainly that this unity will have a direct impact on the world's faith in Christ: "That they also may be one in Us, that the world may believe that You sent Me" (John 17:20).

Therefore, we can plainly say that the power resulting from the unity of the churches is a power to evangelize the world that will preach to the world silently: "There is no speech nor language. Their line has gone out through all the earth" (Ps. 19:4). This is the matter which has caused the Church much toil to this day. The Church, in the past, had desired to reveal herself to the world through the abuse of the words of Christ. However, in the mystical and divine unity

TRUE UNITY WILL BE AN INSPIRATION...

needed for the churches, Christ will reveal Himself to the world through churches' unity in divine love. It is as if unity will be accomplished through the death of the ego of each church, so that the being of Christ may live in them all. A power of resurrection will then burst forth from the Church before and towards the world, the same power in which Christ was raised. In this united Church, Christ will resurrect and be seen by all people. In this manner, Christ awaits the fulfillment of this unity with its voluntary and involuntary conditions, that He may be revealed to the world. It is as if Christ, because of these divisions, is dead, hidden from the world as a buried man in the coldness of animosities and divisions among the churches. Christ waits, and the world waits along with Him, for the end of these divisions, that the warmth of love may spread and, through its spreading, Christ may rise and give life that all may see Him and the world may live on and not die:

> Because I live, you will live also. At that day you will know that I am in My Father, and you in Me, and I in you. He who has My commandments and keeps them, it is he who loves Me. And he who loves Me will be loved by My Father, and I will love him and manifest Myself to him (John 14:19-21).

We truly believe that the world will see Christ as He is (cf. 1 John 3:2), be purified, and, drawn unto Him, follow Him through the purified Church that lives in Christ and the Father and keeps the commandment of unity and love. Did God not love the world and sacrifice His only Son that the world may not perish? (cf. John 3:16). Did Christ not assume human flesh from the world and unite this flesh to Himself to ensure the world's subsistence in a mystical communion and attachment to God? Did God not entrust the mystery of His body unto the Church in order that she may be responsible for this communion and the continuation of this attraction?

The Main Obstacle before Unity

In the unofficial meetings which have taken place between the Chalcedonian and non-Chalcedonian churches till now,[5] it seemed as if the disagreement around Christology and defining who He is can be resolved through a common statement which would be sufficient to begin the process of unity. In my opinion, this sequence will not work. The Gospel points to a similar situation that proves this view to be mistaken. One day a short while before the cross, Christ asked His disciples, "Who do you say I am?" The disciples agreed through the tongue of Peter in one common statement defining the dogma concerning the person of Christ. The contents of this statement were truly wondrous, in agreement with the Orthodox faith, and were even inspired directly by God, as Christ witnessed:

> Simon Peter replied, 'You are the Christ, the Son of the living God.' And Jesus answered him, 'Blessed are you, Simon Bar-Jonah! For flesh and blood has not revealed this to you, but my Father who is in heaven' (Matt. 16:15-17).

---

[5] The article was written in 1984, following four unofficial meetings and a year prior to the first official meeting (1985).

TRUE UNITY WILL BE AN INSPIRATION...

However, it is unfortunate that this Orthodox statement inspired from heaven could not aid the disciples to become united in anything, whether in thought or in practical faith in Christ, nor did it affect the one who said it himself. Peter denied knowing Christ, the disciples were scattered each to his own, and some have gone back to their previous occupations. This was before the descent of the Holy Spirit on Pentecost day. We even hear that they quarreled over who is the greatest (cf. Luke 22:24). Clearly, the careful unanimous formulation of faith, even if inspired by the heavenly Father concerning Christ, is not sufficient for the unity of the disciples nor the churches in their communion in Christ, work, love, sacrifice, and death with Him.

It is truly ironic that in the same chapter in which Peter expressed the right confession concerning Christ, he behaved in a manner that made Christ say to him:

> Get behind me, Satan! You are a hindrance to me. For you are not setting your mind on the things of God, but on the things of man (Matt. 16:23).

Is it not evident that *orthodoxy* does not result naturally in the *orthopraxy*? "You are the Christ, the Son of the living God," and then Christ replied, "You are not setting your mind on the things of God, but on the things of man." This made Christ recognize the gap between faith and behavior, putting the commandment of reconciliation between them; "If anyone would come after me, let him deny himself and take up his cross and follow me" (Matt. 16:24). But the disciples, despite that, returned to ask Christ, "Who is the greatest in the kingdom of heaven?" (Matt. 18:1). As a result, Christ repeated the formula of reconciliation in an even more positive manner, "Unless you are converted and become as little children, you will by no means enter the kingdom of heaven" (Matt. 18:3).

In this manner, it becomes apparent that a united formulation of the Orthodox faith, agreed upon by all, will not be sufficient as an instrument for real unity between the churches, even if it is an essential matter. The divisions have taken spiritual, egoistic, ethnic, worldly, and even political dimensions. Christ is not like that, neither did we know Him to be as such. Thus, our behavior toward Christ differs from the reality of Christ. These are the poisonous roots of division that will continue to feed the division and separation, no matter how beautiful and sound our agreed statements of faith are, like the statement of Peter.

The churches' state is now even more difficult than that of the disciples at the time before the descent of the Holy Spirit upon them. The disciples were in mere doubt, "Who is the greatest in the kingdom of heaven?" (Matt. 18:1). On the contrary, the churches today have reached a state of certainty in this matter. Each church perceives herself as the greatest in the kingdom of heaven with no need for discussion, because she possesses the most accurate and precise faith. As for the needed denial of the self that should accompany faith and the return to the heart and conscience of the children in the strength of the simple faith in Christ, it is a matter—we are afraid and ashamed to say—that cannot be applied to our churches today. Moreover, there is no one in any church delegated to accomplish this task of self-denial.

Therefore, we are missing the Church which can behave in the manner Christ behaved: deny herself, carry her cross, and die to the sin of division, that she may live and cause others to live with her. The most dangerous and absent aspect of churches today is "Christ Himself and Him crucified" (1 Cor. 2:2). The missing element in this instance is exactly this: which of these churches can take upon herself the sins of the past to lift from herself and the others the sin of the present—i.e., division and laceration—for the accomplishment of unity and reconciliation as well as the triumph of love? Speaking of voluntary death, accepting humiliation and crucifixion is difficult. Who can understand this? This case is identical to that of the disciples, when Christ spoke of the necessity of humiliation and the cross in His life:

> 'Behold, we are going up to Jerusalem, and all things that are written by the prophets concerning the Son of Man will be accomplished. For He will be delivered to the Gentiles and will be mocked and insulted and spit upon. They will scourge Him and kill Him. And the third day He will rise again.' But they understood none of these things; this saying was hidden from them, and they did not know the things which were spoken (Luke 18:31-34).

The voice of St. Paul will be of great use in our dialogues around unity as he says, "For I determined not to know anything among you except Jesus Christ and Him crucified" (1 Cor. 2:2). This is to say we ought to move forward with the Spirit of our Lord Jesus, where each church carries the sins of the other church upon herself concurrently and reciprocally. We say: 'Let each church carry the sins of the other church,' without adding anything more.

As for the unofficial meetings and the dialogues of churches which have taken place for decades with much labor, attempts of unity, and suggestions worthy of respect, they can never provide the motivation for each church to take up a Christ-like stand, carrying the faults of others. This matter is greater than intellectual dialogues, extended meetings, and rational solutions, for the churches are confronted with old excommunications. The churches gather in the official absence of the Holy Spirit. Therefore, such meetings have become nothing beyond uncovering the wounds of the past to inflict more suffering.

The Role of the Holy Spirit in Unofficial Meetings

The churches gather and officially declare their meetings unofficial. Why is there such insistence on their meetings to be declared unofficial? Is it because the official churches do not want to abide by the outcomes of these meetings? Or is it that no delegate may deviate even a nudge from the canons of their church and her tradition? Is it because no delegate can concede on any given situation or confess a mistake that was made by their own church in the past or present? Or is it that no delegate may confess the true position of the other church, or that they may not forgive the sin of others? More importantly, in the end, is it because no delegate may have the authority to lift the anathemas and give absolution for the other church?

In other words, the churches insist that their delegates gather informally so that they may continue to assemble in the official absence of the Holy Spirit, thereby preserving the status quo. This condition bears resemblance to the assembly of the disciples in the upper room, where they were divided and terrified as the entrances were sealed. The Holy Spirit is absent, Christ is dead in the tomb, and the Resurrection has

TRUE UNITY WILL BE AN INSPIRATION...

not been revealed yet! As for the disciples, they feared all things, and they feared the Jews, while their Teacher was absent.

Who are the churches afraid of now? Why do they lock their minds' doors? Christ has destroyed the enmity of the most established regulations, canons, and traditions in the world, namely the enmity between the Jews and the Gentiles. He made the two into one, in thought, heart, spirit, and worship. He even destroyed the eternal veil which separated God Himself from humanity and reconciled the heavenly with the earthly, as He destroyed the gates of Hades and set free the imprisoned souls under the authority of Satan. After all of this, are the churches allowed to erect barriers and place locks and shut the doors upon themselves or others? Even after the resurrection has been revealed and Christ appeared with the wounds on His hands and side, giving them peace, the disciples returned to their former life and the mindset of fear and hesitation. Some doubted while others left the group and returned to their old occupation, i.e., catching fish.

In the unofficial meetings, we see the delegates concerned with the exact formulation of the statement of faith for unity. In the light of the above, we see that even if Christ Himself appeared in their midst, and they touched Him, lingering doubt would still be a possibility. Departing from the unanimity remains a likely possibility, for the element of unity which is given by the Holy Spirit is absent. It is the Holy Spirit alone who is in charge of the destruction of all that is old and obsolete in our mind and heart, that is, all that is in disagreement with the love of Christ and all that inhibits the Church's moving forward toward the path of eternal life. He alone is able to loosen the ties and cuffs that inhibited the unity of the Church and delayed her ministry in the world in a sad manner, granting the devil all the chances for a lengthy period of time to plunder in all directions. It seems as if the world needs to initiate a new era that comes with a new birth.

Submission to the Holy Spirit has become a matter of necessity that we may reach the most optimal chances not only for peace and reconciliation but also to start a new leaven in the world for a new life. The division and tearing in the world have spread to the depths of our thought, spirit, and heart and the institutions themselves, so much so that the submission of the churches to the authority of the Holy Spirit has become the most critical and daunting task the churches face since their foundation.

This submission represents the final battle with the power of the devil who is about to divide and shatter everything in the world for destruction: "Every kingdom divided against itself is brought to desolation, and every city or house divided against itself will not stand" (Matt. 12:25). From the beginning, the Church was in principle responsible for kindling the fire of the Holy Spirit into the world: "You are the light of the world" (Matt. 5:14). What is this light but the everlasting spiritual values and the oneness of spirit and works of love? If these spiritual values are absent and the oneness in spirit has been divided and the energy of love scattered between the divisions of churches, who will be able to stand up against the spirit of evil and deception? How will the voice of the world's groaning reach God?

The world, inherently, lacks knowledge of God and can only come to know Him through the Church's works. The Church offers God to the world, not through convincing words, but in demonstration of the Spirit (cf. 1 Cor. 2:4) and

TRUE UNITY WILL BE AN INSPIRATION...

the power of His salvific acts—the manifestations of love, godliness, and self-control, which will inspire and redirect the world.

Love is the unceasing, concealed energy of the Church, but it will not pour on the world except through the oneness of spirit and heart.

The Church cannot offer the world these energies and everlasting values through prominent theologians alone but also through simple, exemplary holy people. The Holy Spirit loves the saints, and through them, He creates the Church of Christ: "And you also will bear witness, because you have been with Me from the beginning" (John 15:27).

Therefore, regardless of how we put the responsibility of unity on the Church, it falls at the end on the shoulders of the saints. If we seek a prompt start, our eyes are fixed on the chosen and gifted in every Church, no matter how much they hide to disappear from the center stage.

IN THE MEANING OF UNITY:

WILL THESE DAYS RETURN?

A heartfelt letter—filled with unwavering devotion,[1] steadfastness, and a profound sense of modesty and humility—exchanged between Julius, Bishop of Rome (337-352), and Athanasius, Bishop of Alexandria (328-373), to celebrate the latter's return from exile.

> Julius, the bishop, to the presbyters, deacons, and people inhabiting Alexandria, brethren beloved, salutations in the Lord.
>
> I also rejoice with you, beloved brethren, because you at length see before your eyes the fruit of your faith. For that this is really so, any one may perceive in reference to my brother and fellow-prelate Athanasius, whom God has restored to you, both on account of his purity of life, and in answer to your prayers. From this it is evident that your supplications to God have unceasingly been offered pure and abounding with love; for mindful of the divine promises and of the charity connected with them, which you learned from the instruction of my brother, you knew assuredly, and according to the sound faith which is in you clearly foresaw that your bishop would not be separated from you

---

[1] First published in December 1975. Mattā al-Miskīn, "Hal ta'ūd haḍihi al-ayyām," in *al-Wiḥda al-masīḥiyya fī ḍaw' ma'nā al-kanīsa wa-ḥaqīqat al-masīḥ* (Wādī al-Naṭrūn: Monastery of Saint Macarius, 2014⁴): 30-33.

WILL THESE DAYS RETURN?

forever, whom you had in your devout hearts as though he were ever present.

Wherefore it is unnecessary for me to use many words in addressing you, for your faith has already anticipated whatever I could have said; and the common prayer of you all has been fulfilled according to the grace of Christ.

I therefore rejoice with you, and repeat that you have preserved your souls invincible in the faith. And with my brother Athanasius I rejoice equally; because, while suffering many afflictions, he has never been unmindful of your love and desire; for although he seemed to be withdrawn from you in person for a season, yet was he always present with you in spirit.

Moreover, I am convinced, beloved, that every trial which he has endured has not been inglorious; since both your faith and his has thus been tested and made manifest to all. But had not so many troubles happened to him, who would have believed, either that you had so great esteem and love for this eminent prelate, or that he was endowed with such distinguished virtues, on account of which also he will by no means be defrauded of his hope in the heavens? He has accordingly obtained a testimony of confession in every way glorious both in the present age and in that which is to come.

For having suffered so many and diversified trials both by land and by sea, he has trampled on every machination of the Arian heresy; and though often exposed to danger in consequence of envy, he despised death, being protected by Almighty God, and our Lord Jesus Christ, ever trusting that he should not only escape the plots of his adversaries, but also be restored for your consolation, and bring back to you at the same time greater trophies from your own conscience.

WILL THESE DAYS RETURN?

By which means he has been made known even to the ends of the whole earth as glorious, his worth having been approved by the purity of his life, the firmness of his purpose, and his steadfastness in the heavenly doctrine, all being attested by your unchanging esteem and love.

He therefore returns to you, more illustrious now than when he departed from you. For if the fire tries the precious metals (I speak of gold and silver) for purification, what can be said of so excellent a man proportionate to his worth, who after having overcome the fire of so many calamities and dangers, is now restored to you, being declared innocent not only by us, but also by the whole Synod?

Receive therefore with godly honor and joy, beloved brethren, your bishop Athanasius, together with those who have been his companions in tribulation. And rejoice in having attained the object of your prayers, you who have supplied with meat and drink, by your supporting letters, your pastor hungering and thirsting, so to speak, for your spiritual welfare.

And in fact you were a comfort to him while he was sojourning in a strange land; and you cherished him in your most faithful affections when he was plotted against and persecuted.

As for me, it makes me happy even to picture to myself in imagination the delight of each one of you at his return, the pious greetings of the populace, the glorious festivity of those assembled to meet him, and indeed what the entire aspect of that day will be when my brother shall be brought back to you again; when past troubles will be at an end, and his prized and longed-for return will unite all hearts in the warmest expression of joy. This feeling will in a very high degree extend to us, who regard it as a token of divine favor that we should have been privileged to become acquainted with so eminent a person.

It becomes us therefore to close this epistle with prayer. May God Almighty and his Son our Lord and Savior Jesus Christ afford you this grace continually, thus rewarding the admirable faith which you have manifested in reference to your bishop by an illustrious testimony: that the things most excellent which 'Eye has not seen, nor ear heard, neither have entered into the heart of man; even the things which God has prepared for them that love him,' (1 Cor. 2:9) may await you and yours in the world to come, through our Lord Jesus Christ, through whom be glory to God Almighty for ever and ever, Amen.

I pray that you may be strengthened, beloved brethren.[2]

Considered as a significant document in history of the relations between the bishops of Alexandria and Rome, this letter serves as an exemplary model for the relations between churches and church leaders. The following elements characterize the letter:

a)   The Christian spirit sprouts from this letter to describe an unparalleled harmony between human feelings and those relating to faith. It is not only belief in the right dogma and faith that dictated this letter, but also the genuine human feelings which evaluated the oppression and persecution that befell an innocent person. The Church is in utmost need of this harmony between theology and humanity.

---

[2] Socrates Scholasticus, *The Ecclesiastical History*, II: 23. Cf. Philip Schaff and Henry Wace (ed.), *Nicene and Post-Nicene Fathers*, Second Series, Vol. 2. (Buffalo, NY: Christian Literature Publishing Co., 1890): 50-1.

b) The kind-hearted bishop who wrote this letter avoided all phrases related to political tones, which basically stem from the 'ego' and the exalting of racial supremacy. He extolled Athanasius as a better person and likewise commended the people of Alexandria as a holier congregation in an amazing humility. In doing so, he exalted himself, without noticing, above all human levels.

c) Likewise, in this letter, we find this honorable bishop has left his soul and emotions to speak of what he feels and believes in faithfulness, sincerity, and simplicity that captures the attention. He spoke with words that would fall short if measured against Roman supremacy. However, if his words are measured with the measure of Christ, his words will be found whole to the fullness of the stature of Christ Himself.

Read also from the same series
ECCLESIA

His Body
The Church Immortal

MATTHEW THE POOR

FOREWORD BY
MET. SABA (ISPER)

*Archbishop of New York
and Metropolitan of the Antiochian
Orthodox Archdiocese of North America*

What is the Church? Is the Church merely a gathering of believers in a place at a certain time, as some scholastics may say? Is the Church just feasts, liturgies, candles, incense, and praises, as some liturgists perceive her? No. The Church is the mystical body of Christ, the continuation of the divine incarnation and the indwelling of the Holy Spirit. She is made of living members forming the true temple of worship. Just as the tree with all its subtle structure is latent in a small seed, she moved from the copies of truth to truth itself; from a tent and temple to a living body; from stones, marble, and gold into believing souls, truth, and faith.

AVAILABLE ON ALL AMAZON STORES, OR ON OUR WEBSITE

www.stmacariuspress.com
info@stmacariuspress.com

www.ingramcontent.com/pod-product-compliance
Lightning Source LLC
Chambersburg PA
CBHW031414040426
42444CB00005B/562